Dealing
with Death
and Dying

Nursing77 Books
Intermed Communications
Jenkintown, Pa.

Dealing with Death and Dying

NURSING77 BOOKS

PUBLISHER: Eugene W. Jackson
Editorial Director: Daniel L. Cheney
Clinical Director: Margaret Van Meter, RN
Circulation Director: Ronald S. Moyer

NURSING77 SKILLBOOK SERIES

SERIES EDITOR: Patricia S. Chaney
Copy Editor: Jane Benner
Production Manager: Bernard Haas
Production Assistants: Debbie Lugar, Margie Tyson
Designer: John C. Isely
Art Director: Matie Patterson
Art Assistants: Maggie Arnott, Patricia Wertz
Cover and divider photographs by John Oldenkamp

ABOUT THE AUTHORS

Sheila Lelly Blake, RN, BS, is Coordinator of Oncology Nursing at Grady Memorial Hospital, Atlanta. She previously worked as oncology research nurse and as instructor in the School of Nursing at Grady Memorial Hospital.

Jeanne Brimigion, RN, is Director of Nursing Services at the Nursing Home and ECF of White Plains, N.Y. She has worked extensively with the elderly in her present job and in general and private duty in hospitals in the White Plains area.

Margaret O'Keefe Diran, RN, MA, is Assistant Professor of Nursing at Staten Island Community College in New York. Her previous positions include head nurse of the thoracic medical-surgical unit at Queens Hospital Center and staff nurse on the pediatric chemotherapy unit at Memorial Hospital, New York.

V. Ruth Gray, RN, MSN, is Assistant Professor of Nursing at Kent State University School of Nursing, Kent, Ohio. She also has conducted grief workshops at Deaconess Hospital, Cleveland. In addition to authoring two chapters, Ms. Gray contributed to the Skillchecks in this book.

Robert E. Kavanaugh, PhD, is Counseling Psychologist at the University of California, San Diego. As an ex-priest, psychologist, and teacher, he has had innumerable contacts with the dying and bereaved.

Ora Prattes, RN, BS, is Project Director of the Barrio Comprehensive Child Care Center in San Antonio, Texas. Her experience also includes supervision of the pediatric units at Robert B. Green Hospital in San Antonio and at Bexar County Hospital.

Eileen Rinear, RN, worked closely with families of the dying in her former position as patient care coordinator at St. Agnes Hospital, Philadelphia. She also has served as an instructor in the St. Agnes Hospital School of Nursing.

Jane C. Williams, RN, MSW, currently serves as Chairperson of Health Occupations at Moraine Park Technical Institute, Fond du Lac, Wisc. She developed a proposal for a death and dying course while a student at University of Wisconsin, Madison, and has participated in several conferences on death and dying. Ms. Williams contributed to the Skillchecks in this book.

Eleanor Gentner, RN, former nurse specialist at Albert Einstein Medical Center, Philadelphia, served as special consultant for the Skillchecks in this book.

Contents

Death and dying. As many people have observed, we health professionals were stashing that subject in the closet with other "unseemly" topics as recently as 10 years ago. Today, we are taking a more open and realistic view of it.

As healthy as this new openness has been, though, it has created a raft of problems for nurses, the health professionals most intimately involved with the dying. Because, despite the proliferation of thanatology literature, few books have addressed the question: Just what is the nurse's role in dealing with death and dying? Fewer still have given nurses concrete answers to such plaguing and perplexing questions as, "What do I say when a patient asks if he's going to die?" And almost none have given nurses a chance to practice dealing with death and dying in risk-free hypothetical situations before they're thrown into frighteningly real life-and-death situations.

Hence, this book — an amalgam of views that attempts to remedy all three deficiencies.

DEALING WITH DEATH AND DYING doesn't attempt to grapple with the theoretical side of thanatology — the pros and cons of euthanasia, for example, or theological orientations. (The fourth section, however, does give you a chance to explore your opinions on such subjects and compare them with those of thousands of other nurses.)

Instead, this book single-mindedly tackles the practical problems of thanatology — how to deal directly with the feelings and fears of the patient, the family, yourself, and other staff members. And it provides several "Skillcheck" questions to let you practice dealing with them.

Although the "Skillchecks" are designed to help you develop your skills while reading this book, you can also use them as prototypes for solving real problems in the future. If you feel stymied by a particularly baffling problem with a patient or family, for example, writing it down as a "Skillcheck" should help you describe and analyze the situation more objectively. In most cases, this new perspective will make the best approach more readily apparent to you.

DEALING WITH DEATH AND DYING certainly isn't intended to reduce your relationships with the dying and bereaved into a neat science; after all, 90 percent of helping depends on warmth and feeling, which can't be taught in any book. But it does suggest some specific guidelines. And those should make the thinking — maybe even the feeling — a little easier.

Introduction: A letter on death from Elisabeth Kübler-Ross

Dear Friend:

It is very late at night, my children are asleep, and I sit alone. I want to talk to you, to try answering your questions — questions like those nurses ask of me at every workshop I run or lecture I give on death and dying. Of course I know nothing about your personal life, as you know nothing about mine. But I feel as if I know you well. I know and can identify with your problems, mostly because many of them are mutual, and partly because I'm a woman, a mother, and a housewife.

Today was typical, punctuated by the innumerable phone calls that have become part of my life. Early today someone asked me to run a workshop this fall, and I had to tell him I'm booked solid for a year (horrible thought). A man called to seek help for himself and his terminally ill wife. A mother whose son is dying in Detroit dropped by because she has no one else to talk to (a sad reflection on our society). My neighbor told me my weeds are taller than my beets and carrots and are almost outgrowing my corn. Just as I was wondering what to cook for dinner, a newly widowed young woman came in. She wanted to talk, and how could I say no to her? When my husband called to say he'd be late for dinner, I felt grateful to him. This, mind you, was supposed to be my day off! The day I thought I'd be able to work on a book manuscript. Well, so it goes, and the day is over, and I find myself sitting at my desk, thinking about those questions nurses have asked me countless times.

• "What do I do if a terminally ill patient wants to talk about his condition, but his doctor and family insist he be kept in ignorance of it? If he says 'Am I going to die?' can I answer with the truth? If not, what answer can I give?"

• "How can I get a physician to level with me, or a social worker, or anybody who can try to help the patient?"

• "When I'm forced to pretend a patient is not dying, how can I successfully relate to him? Constantly making up evasive answers goes against the grain."

Well, we both know these are questions *born of frustration*, and there is no simple, always applicable answer to any of them. Each situation differs. You have to play it more or less by ear. Still, I think that in a way I can help you arrive at answers by calling attention to the fact that, although you're a nurse, you're not *only* a nurse. Being a nurse is only one part of you. You're not a machine but a human being with your own expectations, disappointments, likes, and dislikes. You have many roles, just as I have — a point I tried to illustrate by sharing my day with you. You have to learn to separate these roles, to set priorities and, above all, refuse to let yourself be overwhelmed by anything. Let's look for a moment at the nurse's role as one "average" nurse actually lives it.

She has to serve the physician's needs; she has to please the supervisor, make notes, prepare charts, check medication, and above all (hopefully) take care of patients. But she is also a woman with a private life of her own. She may have children at home with chickenpox, she may be thinking about what to cook for dinner, she may be worrying about her husband's drinking. In other words, when she comes to work she brings all her frustrations, worries, and conflicts with her.

But she will usually be able to separate herself from this private world when she gets to the ward. If all is well there, things will go smoothly. But Mrs. B in 209 may be failing, Mr. K complaining about increasing pain, Miss L may castigate her because she didn't respond fast enough to her call for another shot, which was not due until half an hour later. To make things worse, the resident was late in making rounds, and avoided questions from all but a few terminally ill patients. She is angry with that snobbish so-and-so and knows she's going to be put on the spot when she returns to the patients' rooms. They're going to ask *her* what they really wanted to ask him. She is tempted to tell them the truth. It would serve Dr. S right. "How long does he think *I* can play this game with *his* patients?"

She still feels angry and bewildered when she walks into Mr. K's room. He is crying. She has never seen him cry. On the verge of tears herself (but she won't cry; they'd blame her for being unprofessional!) she sits down next to Mr. K. Between sobs and tears he tells her he's just been told he has cancer and nothing can be done for him. He feels without hope and in a state of impotent rage. He holds on to her, staring at her as if saying, "Do something. Tell me it's not true."

Suddenly her own problems seem trivial. Feeling almost as if someone else were speaking, she hears herself say calmly, "Relax for a minute if you can; then tell me step by step what happened to you." Mr. K sighs deeply, and then, without tears, starts talking. He tells her about his gradually declining health, his vain attempts to believe he was not so sick. After he signed into the hospital, he knew, as test followed test, that all was not well. Today, he was supposed to be told. He was, but not the way he wanted to be. He needed not only truth, but also hope. Most of all, he needed someone to sit by him.

Mr. K felt greatly relieved that he'd had this emotional outburst before his young wife came to visit. He wanted to prepare her slowly and gradually. When the nurse left, he felt he had an ally, a real friend for whom he didn't have to paste on the make-believe smile he presented to his family, who were not yet ready to hear the verdict.

The nurse left Mr. K's room with a great sense of fulfillment and gratification. She was less tired somehow, less angry. Yes, Dr. S had done a poor job when he told the news to Mr. K. But that wasn't entirely his fault. She began to realize that physicians are trained to cure, to treat, to prolong life. But who teaches them how to deal with patients who are beyond help?

As she walked down the hall she saw Dr. S coming out of grouchy Miss L's room. He looked grim and unhappy. Spontaneously she did something she'd never done before. She touched him on the shoulder and said, "Tough, isn't it?"

After a moment of surprise he smiled and said, "God, if you only knew what it's like. All day long I see patients who are not going to get well. I keep thinking, 'What am I doing here? Where are all my dreams of curing people? So I've just prescribed another chemotherapy. What for? To prolong somebody's agony?'" They continued talking as they walked to the nursing station. But the conversation was almost a monologue on his part. He no longer seemed the snob she'd always seen him as. He had, she found, his own dreams, his own disappointments, which he now, for the first time, shared with her. Why had it taken so long? she wondered. They had worked together for months, but each, as if in separate towers, was confined within a role: nurse, doctor.

Their tour of duty over, they went to a little room adjacent to the nurses' station and had coffee together. A social worker joined them, the chaplain looked in, and before long another nurse and an aide came by. They began to talk about what to do with Miss M, a patient who had not yet been told she'd never get well.

This was the founding of the "screaming room" — a room the staff would use from now on, not to give comfort to patients or families, but to themselves. When rounds were too late or too short, when a difficult patient was giving someone trouble, when people just felt they'd "had it," this was the place to come and get support from colleagues. It was a room to cry in. One day the nursing supervisor came in and shared her bitter frustrations. What a difference *that* made.

Sure, there were still many physicians who did not tell their dying patients the truth. But from then on the nurse felt comfortable, because she'd learned that she didn't have to give the patient his diagnosis. (They'd decided this was the physician's responsibility.) But she knew also that, far from being a waste of time, it was all right for her to sit down and *listen*. She knew she could help the patient even if the doctor was copping out. When she was afraid she'd gone too far, she'd visit the screaming room to "confess" to others on the staff. They understood, and would bolster her sagging morale.

Well, I hope that, indirect though my response has been, I've helped indicate the answers to your questions. I guess there's no way to learn but the hard way. *That's the way I learned.* My best teachers were my dying patients. If you dare to get involved, if you dare to sit down and help them go through the stages of dying, they will help you learn not only to become comfortable in caring for them, but also to face, one inescapable day, your own death with dignity. That is, perhaps, their "goodbye gift" to you.

Have I sounded too sad, too gloomy? I hope not. I urge you to live every day to the fullest. "Work when you work, and play when you play" is an old saying I learned to respect a long time ago. In terms of *our* work, it means you should spend a few hours a day with a critically ill or difficult patient. But it also means you should be able to leave the ward, the hospital, the anguish and pain behind you. You have to learn early to switch gears, to enjoy the garden, a boyfriend, whatever makes you happy. You owe that to yourself, your family, and — not least of all — your patients. Hoard the sunshine things in life. You will then be able to spread some of that sunshine in those hospital rooms where it's so desperately needed.

Love and peace,

Elisabeth K. Ross, MD

Elisabeth Kübler-Ross

Dealing with the patient

Some physiological needs

V. RUTH GRAY

FOR ALL MANKIND, living becomes dying; death is the inevitable consequence of living. Yet inevitability does not bring acceptance, willingness, or even comprehension. As a famous French philosopher said, "One cannot look directly at either the sun or death." And, as a psychiatrist, K. Eissler, said, "Which is really harder, to die or to witness death? To some, this question may sound cynical and hypocritical; nevertheless, it has its justification when the contact with the dying is an intimate one."

All of us have emotional problems with death. All of us, in varying degrees, fear death — or, at least, feel concern about our own health. It's only natural that these fears and concerns are heightened by contact with the dying. Our almost automatic reaction is to get away from this most unpleasant situation, which serves only to remind us that one day, we too will have to die.

But nurses, because of our inherent duties, are continually confronted with the reality of another person's dying or death. This confrontation is often painful or difficult, and we must alleviate our feelings of tension and discomfort because we must meet the needs of the dying patient.

What are these needs? We'll discuss them in a few minutes,

but consider this: a nurse who works with dying patients learns of patients' specific needs primarily by listening and looking. We, the living, are forced to enter the dying person's world, to see things through his eyes, to listen to all he can tell us of the experience that remains unique and yet universal to all of us. When we do this — when we identify closely with the patient — we find that death can be kind and filled often with a peace and serenity that escapes the living. For the fear that overshadows our attitude toward the dying comes from our intensive involvement, from our involvement with doing and with curing. The moment a nurse working with the dying goes beyond the role of simply caring for the patient and begins to probe the meaning of death, she will begin to move beyond the defeat that death seems to bring — and move into the arena of hope, joy, and growth.

To enter the dying person's world, you must differentiate between the *process* of dying and the *act* of dying. As Weisman and Hackett, two psychiatrists, put it, "The fear of death is a specific attitude toward the process of dying and is not related to the fact of death."

Dying is the road one travels toward nonbeing, toward physical annihilation. Dying spans a time that may be fraught with pain, bodily impairment, and mental anguish. Death is the actual state of nonbeing. Man cannot conceptualize his own death, his own state of nonentity. He can, however, conceive of the process of dying; he can also conceive of the nonbeing of another person. Thus, *most* persons have a greater dread of the *process* of dying than they do of death itself. Francis Bacon expressed it this way: "I know many wise men that fear to die, for the change is bitter. But I do not believe that any man fears to be dead, but only the stroke of death."

All this brings us to the needs of the dying patient. These needs are (1) psychological or emotional needs, in great measure affected by his stage of dying, and (2) physiological needs affected by his body's adjustments.

In the following chapter, we'll discuss the stages of dying and the patient's psychological needs. But first let's examine his physiological needs.

The sequence of dying   For many years I've observed that there is, for many patients, a sequence of physiological events that relate specifically to the process of dying.

Too often books on death and dying overlook these events and the physiological needs of dying patients; they concentrate solely on the psychological events and needs. True, the psychological needs of a dying patient can be complex and perplexing, and you need to know how to meet them. But I believe that you must know how to meet his physiological needs, too. For by giving planned, purposeful *physical* care, you can begin to convey your understanding of what the patient is experiencing.

● *The patient's sensation and power of motion as well as his reflexes are lost in his legs first and gradually in his arms.* I have observed that pressure on the extremities at this time seems to bother the patient. Sheets should not be snug, or they'll make the patient uncomfortable. He should be turned frequently and given special attention to the positioning of his legs.

● *As peripheral circulation fails, there is a "drenching sweat" and the body surface cools, regardless of room temperature.* The sweating is most profuse on the upper parts of the body and on the extensor surfaces rather than on the flexor surfaces. Body temperatures will begin to rise. Most dying patients are never conscious of being cold, *regardless* of how cold their body surface becomes. Their restlessness is often caused by sensation of *heat.* Their tossing is to throw off bed clothes. At that point they need lighter clothing and fresh circulating air. Oxygen tents will not help. You need to control the environment and explain to relatives that even though their loved one may feel cold to their touch, he is not aware of being cold, because his internal temperature is quite high.

● *The dying patient always turns his head toward the light.* As sight and hearing fail, the dying see only what is near and hear only what is distinctly spoken to them. Indirect lighting should be provided in the room, and the loved one should be seated near the patient at the head of his bedside. Nurses and relatives should never draw the shades in the room, never talk in whispers in a corner, and never fail to answer honestly any of the patient's questions. To do this, as psychiatrists Weisman and Hackett say, we "unwittingly impose the phenomenon of premortem dying."

● *The dying patient's touch sensation is diminished, yet the dying can sense pressure.* You should find out if the patient likes to be touched. Remember, touch can be an intrusion. Some patients may prefer to blink their eyes to communicate. I

To enter the dying person's world, you must differentiate between the *process* of dying and the *act* of dying. Dying is the road one travels toward nonbeing, toward physical annihilation. Dying spans a time that may be fraught with pain, bodily impairment, and mental anguish. Death is the actual state of nonbeing. Man cannot conceptualize his own death. Thus, most persons have a greater dread of the process of dying than they do of death itself.

The dying patient may seem in pain throughout the dying process. If, however, all of his other needs are met and if he is at the stage of acceptance where he has said all he feels he needs to say, he may need minimal pain medication.

recall a patient who said to me, "I've never been a demonstrative person. I don't especially want to die with someone holding my hand, but I don't want to die alone."

• *The dying patient may seem in pain throughout the dying process.* If, however, all of his other needs are met and if he is at the stage of acceptance where he has said all he feels he needs to say, he may need minimal pain medication. If peripheral circulation has failed, his medication should be given intravenously.

• *The dying patient is often conscious to the very end.* And so to the very end, you need to give total care. If the patient is conscious, he is, in dying, the person he was in living. If he was a teacher, a physician, a preacher in life, he will be a teacher, a physician, a preacher when he is dying.

I remember caring for a retired physics teacher who was directing some research with four young college students at the time his malignant tumor was discovered. At surgery, metastatic lesions were found. After surgery he did not do well. He was discharged for a short time, but was readmitted in a terminal stage.

One day, his four students came to visit him and share the exciting news that they had tested and proved their hypothesis. At first, the students were told their professor was too sick and they could not possibly visit. When I questioned that decision, I was told, "The man is too weak to care. And those fellows wouldn't want to see a dying man." I suggested that we leave the decision up to the patient.

I told him his students were there and asked him if he'd like them to visit then or have them return later. He smiled and responded, "Once in a while my mind wanders to that project they are working on. I want to see them." I talked with the students and prepared them for seeing the patient. I mentioned that he looked thin and very frail, and that his voice was barely audible. I encouraged them to go in, stand at the head of his bed, and speak distinctly to him. I asked them not to ask questions that he would have to exert energy answering. They were in the room about 3 minutes, and I shall always feel that the patient profited by the visit as he learned the direction he'd given his students had proved valuable. I think those students grew up a little that day, too.

• *Spiritual needs often arise most strongly at night.* If a patient has had a strong spiritual life, he's apt to want to talk about it and share his experiences with those near him. If he

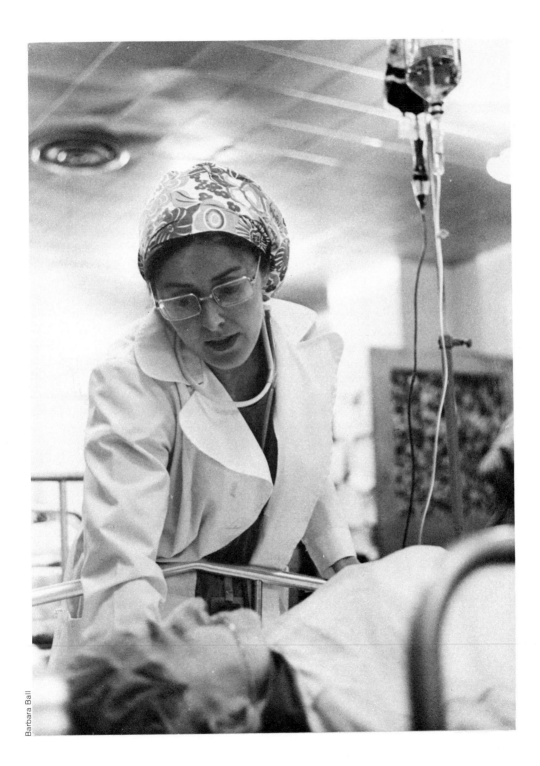

has had questions about his life, those also come out when he is dying. So, he may want to talk about those things — particularly, I've found, in the evening or night hours.

Patients so often ask to talk with their minister, their rabbi, or their priest in the middle of the night. These are times when contacting clergy is difficult. I really think we need to do more to provide spiritual help for patients around the clock. Psychiatrists Weisman and Hackett said, "Only the clergy are qualified to meet spiritual needs of the dying patient." I would agree, perhaps, but in the middle of the night often the nurse must minister to those needs. I think nurses should become comfortable in reading Scripture to patients and their families if they are asked to do so, and in reciting the 23rd Psalm and the Lord's Prayer.

Through the years, I've met some dying patients who radiated beautiful personalities as the result of the kind of life they lived. Although I was raised in a family that read the Bible, I never came to understand the Book of Joshua until I cared for a particular woman. Her husband asked to have selected verses from that chapter read to his wife each night. The verse I read most frequently to her was *Joshua 1:9*, "Have I not commanded you? Be strong and of good courage; be not frightened, neither be discouraged, for the Lord your God is with you wherever you go."

The husband of another dying woman asked that the last paragraph from Kelly's A TESTAMENT OF DEVOTION be read each night:

"Life from the beginning is a life of unhurried peace and power. It is simple; it is serene; it is amazing; it is triumphant. It takes no time, but occupies all our time and makes life's problems new and overcoming. You need not get frantic, for He is at the helm, and when your little day is past, you lie down quietly in peace, for all is well."

• *There seems to be an interval of peace before death, before the final act of life.* Those patients who are conscious to the very last minute answer, invariably, that they do not suffer. As William Hunter, the great anatomist, whispered, just before he died, "If I had strength to hold a pen, I would write how easy and pleasant a thing it is to die."

The psychological response

V. RUTH GRAY

NO TWO PEOPLE react to dying or death in exactly the same way. Yet, much like the *physiological* events of dying, grief, which is the *psychological* response, goes through certain characteristic stages. Knowing what these stages are will help you anticipate and meet the dying patient's psychological needs.

Two authorities have described the stages of grief in a most helpful fashion. One is Dr. George Engel, who described three stages of grief of a relative who has just lost a loved one *(Grief and Grieving,* AMERICAN JOURNAL OF NURSING, Sept. 1964). Another is Dr. Elisabeth Kübler-Ross, who described five stages of grief of a patient who has learned he has a fatal illness (ON DEATH AND DYING, Macmillan, 1969).

Initial shock

Dr. Engel describes the initial response as one of *shock and disbelief.* The one who grieves cannot grasp the reality of what has happened. He may desperately and intensely deny that reality. This is much like the *shock and denial* state described by Dr. Kübler-Ross.

You may have seen this reaction in the parents of a child born with a deformity. They cannot believe that this could happen to their child. I see it sometimes in parents whose infant is born with a cleft lip. Recently I saw it in parents whose two-month-old son, they said, was not eating as well as he should. The child was mongoloid. It was only after our physician made the diagnosis that they admitted being told the same thing at another clinic. They had refused to believe that the diagnosis was correct.

In the same way, the patient who has been told that he has a fatal illness says, "No. It can't be me. It's not possible." He may visit several physicians, hoping the first diagnosis was incorrect.

This shock and denial stage may be accompanied by the physiological reaction to disaster or impending disaster: shock, fainting, pallor, sweating, tachycardia, nausea, gastrointestinal disturbances. Restlessness, confusion, or apathy are common also. Crying may or may not occur. Dr. Kübler-Ross says that denial may vanish if the person in grief knows someone will help him express the feeling that will emerge when he faces reality.

Awareness and anger   Dr. Engel's second stage is that of *developing awareness*. In this stage, reality begins to penetrate the consciousness. The individual will feel sadness mixed with guilt, shame, helplessness, and hopelessness. He will feel a strong urge to cry. "Crying," says Dr. Engel, "seems to fulfill an important homeostatic function." He may now blame himself for something he has failed to do, or he may lash out at society and blame others for what happened to him. He may also feel empty.

Analogous to this stage are Dr. Kübler-Ross' stages of *anger, bargaining, and depression*. The patient progresses from "No, not me!" to "Yes, me, but . . ." to simply "Yes, me."

The angry patient will be difficult to get along with. Whatever you do will be wrong. When you go to bathe the patient, he will want to rest. If you let him rest, he will say he is not being cared for properly. You cannot get his medication to him soon enough. His food, always too hot or too cold, never tastes good. The harder you try, the harder time the patient gives you. Why does this happen? Why does the patient respond in this manner? Dr. Kübler-Ross, after interviewing many patients, found that the more energetic and peppy the nurse, the more anger she provoked in the patient. In essence, the patient was saying, "You can walk out of here and I can't. You can go home after work and see your family and I can't." He is not angry at you yourself, but at the attributes you represent — vitality, freedom, purpose — which he has lost or is about to lose.

A couplet from the Iliad (Pope's translation) eloquently describes the anger born of grief: "Grief tears his heart, and drives him to and fro/In all the raging impotence of woe." When patients are in this stage, you will do them a great service by helping them express their feelings freely. Patients will feel more comfortable, will call upon you less frequently if these expressions are made.

The bargaining ("Yes, me, but . . .") stage described by Dr. Kübler-Ross is characterized by the patient's trying to make a deal with God or fate, promising some act in exchange for more time. "If I'm allowed to live one more year, I'll. . . ." In this stage the patient usually is exhausted and depressed. If his tragic situation is mentioned, he may choke up and feel weak and short of breath. This acute reaction may come in waves and last for 20 minutes to an hour.

From the bargaining stage, the patient progresses to the stage of depression alone. He is quiet, speaks rarely, and discourages visits from friends and relatives. The nurse may find him crying softly or silently mourning. What should she do? She should, Kübler-Ross tells us, allow him time to grieve. In this way he is preparing himself to give up those he loves and the things that have been meaningful to him. Finally, he may want only one loved person to sit silently at his side.

In speaking of the one who has suffered a loss, Dr. Engel describes the final stage of grief as one of *restitution and recovery,* one in which peace and well-being are reattained. The mourner may call on friends and relatives to give him needed support. Several months — Engel says from 6 to 12 — will go by before he is able to think of his loss without sadness. According to Engel, "Complete resolution of grief . . . is indicated by the ability to remember comfortably and realistically both the pleasure and the disappointments of the lost relationship."

Dr. Kübler-Ross sees a similar stage — she calls it *acceptance* — in the dying patient. The patient says, "I have finished all, till now, unfinished business. I've said all the words that had to be said. I am ready to go." It is a good, not

The angry patient will be difficult to get along with. Whatever you do will be wrong. Why does the patient respond in this manner? He is angry not at you yourself, but at the attributes you represent — vitality, freedom, purpose — which he has lost or is about to lose.

Then, acceptance

bitter, feeling. The patient is certainly not happy, but not terribly sad either.

For example, last summer one of our patients was a blind, 63-year-old lady dying from severe congestive heart failure. She had no living relatives, no one to sit by her bed, hold her hand, and wait with her. Yet her face was benignly peaceful. One day a discerning young nurse heard her humming, with what little breath she had, "Swing Low Sweet Chariot." The nurse said, "Would you like to sing a duet?" "Oh yes," the lady said, "I'd love that." And she began singing in a beautiful soprano vibrato that astonished everyone on the ward.

The resident physician said, "I don't know how she can do it, but let her sing if she wants to." The next evening around dinner time she and the nurse sang again. When the food was served, she asked the nurse to say the blessing. Then she asked if she could talk about her life and her Lord, and what He'd meant to her. When she finished, she said, "I'm no earthly good to anyone. I'd just as soon go home, but I did want one last time to share my Lord with someone." Acceptance. Not long after, she calmly and peacefully went from consciousness to coma to death, all in the space of three hours.

Some persistent needs

Shock, anger, acceptance. To help the dying patient move through these stages toward a peaceful death, you must strive to relieve his loneliness, depression, and fears. These considerations will be discussed at length in the next chapter. But here, let's take a general look at some persistent needs.

Whatever his specific illness or situation, every dying patient needs to maintain his security, self-confidence, and dignity. This means you should never leave him isolated or abandoned, which of course is possible in our clinical settings today. And you should help relatives and friends with their emotions relating to death so they will be able to stay with the patient in his time of loneliness and need. You can prepare visitors by describing the kind of day the patient is having and by explaining reasons for any new equipment that might be in the room. If visitors are not prepared, they may become emotionally upset in the patient's presence. In that situation, the patient, instead of receiving help, is the one who has to give help to his relatives.

Visitors often tend to talk in future-oriented conversations with the patient — even though they and the patient know they are fraudulent. It is best, I believe, to avoid clichés such as "Everything is going to work out fine" . . . "You'll be up and about in no time" . . . and "You look fine." The patient usually knows how things are going to work out; he knows he probably won't be up and about; and he certainly knows how he looks.

The same guiding principle should apply to your conversation. You should be so closely in tune with what he is experiencing that even the tone of your voice will convey that you understand what he is experiencing. What an affront to any dying patient for the nurse to come into the room and speak only of the beautiful sunny morning and the gorgeous spring flowers in bloom outside. This may be the nurse's way of coping with her fears of death. But it is devastating to the patient who is dying. *Proverbs 26:20* speaks rather specifically, I think, to this. In modern-day terms, it says: "Being happy-go-lucky around a person whose heart is heavy is as bad as stealing his jacket in cold weather or rubbing salt into his wounds."

The dying patient's opinion should always be sought on current problems if he is physically and mentally able to deal with them.

When he asks about his family, he wants honest answers. He cares as deeply for them when he is dying as he did when he was well. Concern over loved ones can cause a dying patient to feel uneasy and to require more medication and physical care than he might otherwise need.

I shall never forget working with a dying patient who rather quickly turned to me and asked, "Will I die today?" The intern who had just drawn blood from the patient heard his "page" and had to leave the room, and the medication nurse left quickly with her medicine tray. I had known this patient for quite some time and knew he had openly discussed his physical state with me and others. I had learned in morning report that he'd had a restless night and needed more pain medication than usual. Because of the many times I'd talked with him, I sat down at his bedside and replied, "I know that you know that I don't know if you will die today. I also know that you've had a restless night with pain and with little sleep. Is there something troubling you?"

"Well," said he, "when I asked about my grandson last

Visitors often tend to talk in future-oriented conversations with the patient — even though they and the patient know they are fraudulent.
It is best, I believe, to avoid clichés such as "Everything is going to work out fine" . . . "You'll be up and about in no time" . . . and "You look fine." The patient usually knows how things are going to work out; he knows he probably won't be up and about; and he certainly knows how he looks.

A case in point

night, I learned he fractured his arm and is being operated on this morning in another hospital. I love that boy, and I just want to be certain I live long enough to find out if he's okay."

When the other hospital called, we found his grandson had had surgery and was in good condition in the recovery room. This news relaxed the patient. He asked no more questions about dying. And with very little medication, he was able to catch up on the sleep he'd lost the night before.

The dying patient needs to have his loved ones visit. But as he becomes weaker, he may choose to limit visitors to one or two persons dearest and nearest to him. You should get to know these persons well and be sensitive to their needs also. I've found that loved ones do not become so exhausted *physically* and *emotionally* if they can participate to some extent in the patient's care. And of course, such participation may help them in their own grieving process, for they will be able to reflect not only on the support their presence brought to their loved one but also on the comfort their ministrations of care brought.

My own personal hope for nurses and for all members of the health professions who care for the dying is this: that we come to accept and understand the fact that dying is as much a part of life as birth. And when our dying patients say to us, "Tell me, will I die?" we will be able to say forthrightly, "Yes, you will, and so will I."

Allaying common fears

JANE C. WILLIAMS

HOW TO HELP THE DYING? From my experience, these patients have three levels of fear — fear of pain, fear of loneliness, and fear of meaninglessness. One way to help them is to allay these fears.

Fear of pain is one of the most acute and realistic of fears. To help the patient, you need to constantly assure him that he will be kept comfortable with medication and that the health team has not given up on him. And you can do much to comfort the family by assuring them that the final dying itself is usually painless.

As long ago as 1878, in a book called VISIONS, a wise man by the name of Edward Clark wrote, "One of the most common errors is the notion that pain and dying are inseparable companions. The truth is, they rarely go together. Occasionally the act of dissolution is a painful one, but this is an exception to the general rule. The rule is that *unconsciousness,* not pain, attends the final act. To the subject of it, death is no more painful than birth . . . Nature kindly providing an anesthetic for the body when the spirit leaves it."

Loneliness — the second fear — has a profound relationship to pain, for pain is found to be the most intense when the patient is left alone. I remember a young mother whose cancer

From what I've seen and heard, most people die when someone is with them in the room. Isn't it possible that the dying person waits, that he holds onto life, so that he may die in the presence of another human being? Indeed, many people fear going to sleep not because they may die, but because they may die all alone.

had eaten through to her spine, leaving her paralyzed from the waist down. She was in almost constant pain and needed a light treatment to the open area for 45 minutes three times a day. The busy staff would usually prop her up on her side and leave her with the light shining on her spine. Within 5 minutes, she would be screaming with pain. But, when someone would hold her gently on her side and talk with her, she could tolerate the whole treatment with minor discomfort.

I can't emphasize enough how sensitive we need to be to the urgent plea, "Please don't leave me alone." And that plea, you must remember, comes in many forms: verbal and nonverbal, symbolic and direct. I'm thinking, now, of a young husband and father — Ken, 26 — who was dying of Hodgkin's disease. A few days before his death, I was walking past the nurses' station when several staff members stopped me and said I just had to do something, of all things, about Ken's smoking. They said he'd become a chain smoker overnight, that he was too weak to smoke alone and so might start a fire, but that they were too busy to sit with him. His wife, who was denying to herself how seriously ill he was — a defense I will come back to in a later chapter — said she didn't have the time to sit with him. Besides, she didn't want to encourage his smoking because "it wasn't good for his health."

I then went into Ken's room. I sat with him for over an hour, and he never asked to smoke. In fact, I even asked him several times if he wanted to, but he always said no. It didn't take much to figure out what this dying man was saying. He hadn't become a chain smoker. Rather, he knew he couldn't be left alone if he smoked, and so he'd found one way of assuring someone's presence.

From what I've seen and heard, most people die when someone is with them in the room. Isn't it possible that the dying person waits, that he holds onto life, so that he may die in the presence of another human being? Indeed, many people fear going to sleep not because they may *die* but because they may die all *alone*. Think of how many people witness a birth, and what preparation and anticipation surround this event. It would seem fitting that a lifetime is worthy of some ceremony at its final moment, its final act.

Not that it's necessary to engage in elaborate conversation with the dying person. The simple presence of another human being is all he really needs to let him know he is not being abandoned.

In fact, a great deal of a young child's fear of his own death is involved in the idea of "aloneness" — specifically, in separation from mother. We see the tremendous anguish in children on every pediatric ward when Mommy must leave, or when a youngster wakes in the night to see only a strange nurse. Parents should be encouraged to spend time with their terminally ill children and be allowed to touch them and hold them. This calms the child's fears and helps the family work through the adjustment to the tragedy. It also lessens the parents' feelings of uselessness in helping their youngster. Moreover, many observers have found that a youngster will face dying much the same way as his *parents* face his dying. Thus, in helping the family begin working through the process of grieving while the child is still alive, we can enable the child to approach his impending death more comfortably and with less anxiety.

In older patients, the *existential* fear of separation — the ultimate fear of loneliness, so to speak — often expresses itself as hostility toward others: staff, family, significant others, God. We must remind ourselves not to take this hostility personally; furthermore, we should be interpreters to the family of this kind of behavior. The dying need to be given the "permission" to express their anger and hostility, to know that it will be met with support and understanding.

The third level of fear — fear that one's life has been meaningless, or that life itself is meaningless — can be very difficult to relate to and deal with. People seem to search unceasingly for meaning. It would seem that we do not desire to live forever, but that our living be totally meaningful; that what we strive for is not self-preservation but self-fulfillment.

I like to recall a bit of philosophy expressed by Viktor Frankl's concept in MAN'S SEARCH FOR MEANING: "Having been is a kind of being, perhaps the surest kind." That idea reaffirms the importance of an individual's life. It's a way of enabling people to find meaning in suffering and living. It is a way of attaining immortality: by having lived, you become eternal.

Consider the following poignant way an elderly woman struggled to maintain meaning and purpose in the final days of her life.

For long periods of the day, as she lay there in the hospital, she would perform a peculiar ritual: she would keep passing a knotted string between her fingers. The staff said she was

Fear in the young and old

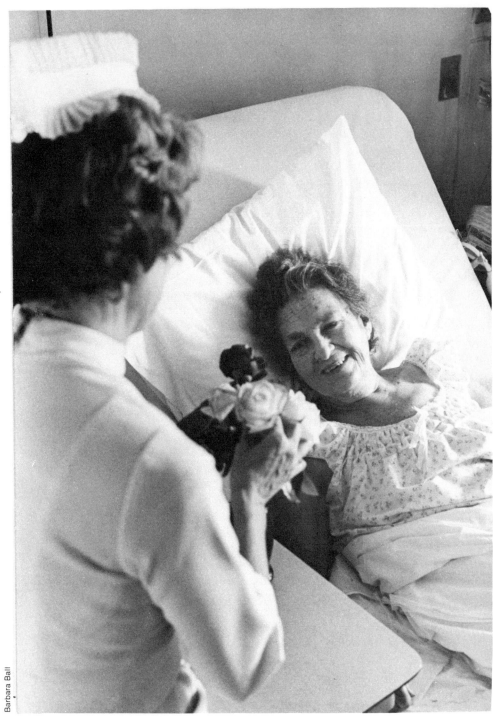

senile, which seems to be our society's usual way of dealing with old age. A young doctor jokingly said it was her way of masturbating. However, when someone sat down with the dying old woman and asked about this strange behavior, the answer was both surprising and beautiful.

"Oh, this string is just the dearest thing to me. My grandmother taught me when I was a little girl to get a new string on each birthday. And then when something good happens, when God smiles on your life and a nice thing happens, you tie a knot in your string. Then when the days are dark and lonely, when despair is very real, then you get out your string and remember the good times. Then the pain isn't so bad." That knotted string was her way of belonging, of having been, of remaining eternal.

Will and hope manifest themselves in our ability to be mobile and in our ability to express ourselves. So, if we can keep a person's will working, if we can enable him to find some meaning or value in life, then his ego strengths will be maintained.

But "having been" is not enough for so many people; as the meaning of their lives slips away, depression rushes in. The best definition of depression I've heard is: "My will won't work." Will and hope manifest themselves in our ability to be mobile and in our ability to express ourselves. When the will works and imagination functions, a person will continue to have purpose. So, if we can keep a person's will working, if we can enable him to excite his imagination to find some meaning or value in life, then his ego strengths will be maintained.

Fear of meaninglessness

It takes a team to work on any large scale with the dying and bereaved. But even though the team may be made up of different types of professionals — doctor, nurse, social worker, clergyman, and others — there should be no rigid division of responsibility in ministering to the dying patient and his family. What happens too often is that each member of the team gets so involved in his own professional interest that he forgets he's a member of a team. Ironically, it seems that the more people who have the opportunity to help the patient and family, the less that gets done. To avoid this, whichever member of the team can establish rapport with a particular patient and his family is the one who should work with them.

The dying patient has so many unmet needs you can fill. You only need to care and to have your head together as to your own feelings, and not be afraid to cry. But often, as you sit with the dying patients, you might wonder: "What is the *right* thing to do?" Perhaps it's most helpful if you would think: "How would *I* feel? What would *I* want said or done?"

To reinforce what I've already said about not needing an elaborate conversation with the patient, I suggest you try to remember a time when you yourself were really down and just prayed for someone who would understand. Chances are, you weren't looking for a lot of talk, but for someone who simply would listen and not be afraid to touch you.

If you can remember such a time, and most of us can, then you will know that you need to leave your "armor of professionalism" outside the door. Patients often feel repulsive, freaky, unclean. Touching them, putting a hand on their hand or on the nape of their neck, can mean so much, can make it a truly caring encounter.

Indeed, there's even a time for humor. All too often we forget that the dying need to have smiles and lightness in their lives. As a dying patient commented to a hospital chaplain, "Since we heard of my diagnosis, you never tell jokes anymore. You are so glum and I miss your humor. You used to be so funny."

I'm not talking about humor used as a "cop-out" for dealing honestly with reality, but rather as one of the normal ways that people relate to one another.

How to help the dying? The following words written by a dying student should both haunt us and point the way: "The dying patient is not yet seen as a person and thus cannot be communicated with as such. He is a symbol of what every human fears and what we each know, at least academically, that we too must someday face . . . . We may ask for whys and wherefores, but we don't really expect answers . . . . If only we could be honest, both admit of our fears, touch one another. If you really care, would you lose so much of your valuable professionalism if you cried with me? Just person to person? Then, it might not be hard to die . . . in a hospital . . . with friends close by."

Children's special needs?

ROBERT E. KAVANAUGH

LAST WEEK, OUR FAMILY buried "Grandma Kitty," my 63-year-old mother-in-law and dear friend. Some of her 17 grandchildren came to the wake, viewing a dead person for the first time. Others could only phone or write their sympathies to "Grandpa Andy." A few made no contact.

Watching those that came and reading the letters of others, I reflected on how similarly children and adults react to death. While I've read and admire the findings of scholars who study children facing death, rarely do I discover any conclusions that couldn't as easily apply to most adults.

At least in part, most of us approach death as children — especially Americans, schooled as we are in an atmosphere that features death in our news and entertainment, but clouds our own death in child-like fantasies of omnipotence and immortality.

Nurses who work with dying children, I believe, can improve their effectiveness and inward peace by reflecting on that cultural heritage.

Like it or not, the child within each of us remains in operation throughout life, especially in areas like dying and death, where our growth has been culturally retarded. Just as we might best learn how to give proper sexual instructions to

Although we all would like to become the fortress that people seem to need and expect around dying, sometimes all we have to offer is our little-child-self. And that child-self wants to run. It fails to grasp final separation. It sees death as a boogeyman, and it flits youthfully from dying to trivia and on to irrelevant subjects. Admitting the childlikeness of our death-related attitudes requires uncommon humility. But if we humbly peel back external pretenses, professional routines and self-protecting styles of dealing with dying children, we can listen and learn with the "child within" as source-book.

children by imparting clear answers to our own personal questions, maybe we could best understand the needs of dying children by consulting the needs of the child within ourselves.

Few of the health care professionals I encounter have a mature and well-balanced attitude toward dying children. I hear their tales of self-heroics and their routine answers, their complicated rationalizations and blame of physicians. I see so much pretending, so much fervent searching for easy paths through grief and so much displaced anger. All of these are attitudes and evasions that we expect from *children* dealing with life and its passing.

Although we all would like to become the fortress that people seem to need and expect around dying, sometimes all we have to offer is our little-child-self. And that child-self wants to run. It fails to grasp final separation. It sees death as a boogeyman, and it flits youthfully from dying to trivia and on to irrelevant subjects.

Admitting the childlikeness of our death-related attitudes requires uncommon humility. After all, our attitudes lie buried under multiple layers of "oughts" and "shoulds" acquired at home and in professional training. But if we humbly peel back some of these external pretenses, these professional routines and self-protecting styles of dealing with dying children, we can listen and learn with the "child within" as source-book.

Our cultural background makes working with dying children difficult because it infuses the word "children" with a magical force. Parents often sacrifice their personal lives and even their marriages on the altar of child worship. "Anything for the children!" The emotional impact of the word keeps dads working too much and moms slaving incessantly.

Any long-term improvement of nursing care for dying children requires a more balanced perspective. Children are not mini-gods; they are simply little persons. They are not a distinct species; they are beginning human beings.

Modern history abounds with stories of children enduring catastrophes side-by-side with adults. They suffered in concentration camps and through atomic bombs. They stood vigil at mine shafts where dads or brothers were trapped. And, until two generations ago, they frequently confronted the deaths of brothers and sisters, of parents or grandparents, in their family homes.

Children would benefit if we would free them from their magical boxes and the overly protective cages in which our cultural fears have locked them. True, some children are fragile. But I also know fragile adults. True, some children would sulk in anger or grow hysterical with fear if we discussed dying and death more openly with them. But on the whole, dealing openly with their feelings is much more humane than leaving them suffering and isolated in their magical boxes.

Our goal must be to see children as one of us. Death is their heritage as well as ours. Reflection on that idea may not overcome our cultural barriers, but it will begin to remove a stumbling block to the more humane and effective treatment of dying children.

The usual books on children and death outline in a general way the growth stages of children, citing their needs and understanding at each phase of development. They state, for example, that preschool children rarely grasp the final separation in death. They see death as "mommy being gone" or as "daddy on a trip." As one terminal four-year-old asked: "Do they have pencils and papers in heaven so I can write letters home?"

Rules fall short

Unfortunately, though, generalities don't solve the daily dilemmas of nurses working with dying children, each of whom is a bundle of quite specific needs. Children grow at such varied paces. They can arrive at new insights daily, even hourly — particularly with such subtle forces as television, games, playmates, hospital roommates, dead cats, and comic books unevenly shaping their understanding and emotional growth. Knowing for certain the emotional level and distinct needs of a particular child can come only with continuing, long-term contact.

Unfortunately, too, the saintly pictures that experts paint of nurses to the dying — and the pressures to "measure up" — do a real disservice to the working nurse. I'm convinced that no "proper" method of treating dying children exists. Each nurse has a charisma, a unique and special way of affecting children, that will naturally attract some and put off others. And personal charisma can't be discovered or developed by trying too hard to model after someone you admire. Internal peace and confidence with terminal children comes only when you bring your true self to the bedside.

Freedom from the need to become "The Six-Million Dollar

Nurse" allows your own consciousness to rise. Gradually you can realize your own problems with death and with dying children. Gradually, too, you can discern the connection — and distinction — between your personal problems and the dying child's problems.

This freedom also will help you see that no two dying children and no two families react exactly alike. Schooled in an aura of prescriptions, orders, and formulae, we naturally seek exact rules or routines for application to dying children and their survivors. But the search is futile. No matter how many times you attend a dying child, no universal formula will always work. And you'll never discover a satisfactory answer to the underlying wonderment that mystifies us all: "Why, oh why must little children suffer and die?"

At best we can sketch general guidelines, which can support us along a path that even the gifted find thorny. These guidelines fall into three areas: First, the needs of the attending nurse. Then, the needs of the dying child. And finally, the needs of the grief-stricken family.

Set guidelines for yourself

Define your role as the child's advocate and informant. In the care of a dying child, you work as a partner with the physician, the family, and other professionals. But the parents and physician retain primary responsibility for informing the child. In some cases, where the parents and physician are reluctant to inform the child, you may be tempted to become a crusader for the child's rights. Although theory holds that each child has a right to know, you'd be wise to avoid the temptation to crusade.

Remember that not all responsible parties simultaneously reach emotional readiness to tell a child. Nurses, particularly pediatric nurses, often possess a special rapport with youngsters and can relate to them more quickly than physicians or even parents. On the other hand, as several pediatric nurses have told me, they often are less able to deal effectively with adults. They tend to write off a reluctant physician or to hold frightened parents at bay with anger or a hint of disdain. The child needs all parties. So, as an understanding nurse, you should work as a catalyst and partner, rather than a crusader and an adversary.

Maintain an abiding respect for your own personal needs. You can't be truly helpful near chronic trauma if you consis-

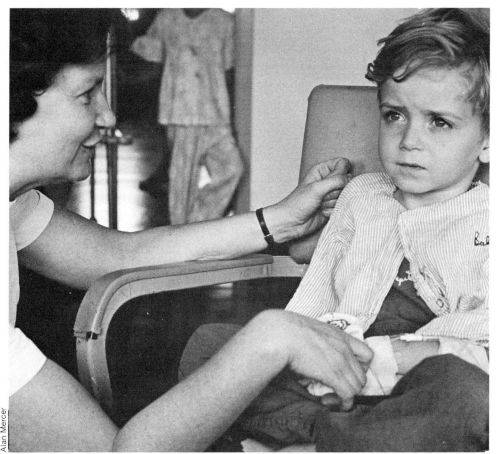

tently overinvest emotionally. The care of dying children demands skill in the art of distancing. To be as open, warm and giving as you can, limited only by your professional duties, your responsibilities to other patients, and the realities of your personal life — this is how I describe the art of distancing. Some days you'll have much to give; other days you'll have only a tiny bit. If several patients are critical, if you feel friction with the staff, or if you have trouble at home, any undue involvement with a dying child may cause all your other tribulations to overflow.

To the idealist, the art of distancing may sound selfish, but it is realistically grounded in self-respect and love for others. As human beings, nurses naturally feel cranky, "hyper," or depressed on some days. We can give to others only from our abundance, and some days the cupboard is bare. But that is okay. We need feel no guilt for being able to provide only a

Remember that not all parties simultaneously reach emotional readiness to tell a child his prognosis. Nurses, particularly pediatric nurses, often possess a special rapport with youngsters and can relate to them more quickly than physicians or even parents.

little when a lot seems warranted. Guiltily running to play super-nurse at the expense of ourselves, our family, our peers, and perhaps our professional future accomplishes nothing. And nothing drives good and sensitive nurses out of traumatic areas of nursing faster than continued emotional overinvestment. Yet, unless a nurse sometimes does overinvest emotionally, she'll never know whether she regularly invests enough of herself. We can master the art of distancing only by experience.

Understand and respect the grieving process as it unfolds within yourself and within all those even peripherally involved with a dying child. Everyone, including the entire health care team, will grieve according to his individual style of coping and according to the extent of his involvement. Some people begin grieving at their first awareness of terminal illness; others don't begin until much later, when they are ready to experience the pain. The child grieves, too, over the loss of those he loves, over loss of freedom and mobility, and maybe over loss of hair or weight or beauty.

While respecting your own grief, you should allow wide latitude for the varied manifestations of grief around you. Remember that grief, always a complex emotion, grows more complex when people feel overextended, helpless, and under public scrutiny. It may produce uncharacteristic behavior or inappropriate reactions when the child is expiring. It may appear as shock or withdrawal, disorganized behavior, depression, guilt, anger, sadness, relief, hysteria, and psychosomatic ailments, to mention only a few manifestations.

The grief-stricken need outlets and emotional support far more than advice. They need to shed tears if they are the crying kind, to explode if they are the exploding kind. Some need to talk or to ramble, while others prefer silence. Some want privacy, while others want an audience. Many want to run, and just as many want to be hugged. A few need to lash out in angry tirades. Above all, each person needs to work through his grief in a highly personal way. And so do you.

I firmly believe that any person who works regularly around the dying needs a companion, one who is readily available for ventilation. Where health care teams exist, companionship comes ready-made, if stuffy professionalism doesn't hamper grieving. Where teams don't exist or where "professionalism" dominates their mission, nurses need to seek out another nurse, an aide, a chaplain, a social worker, or anyone concerned enough to listen. Those who can't find a companion at work need one at home. Not to find one anywhere is to be saddled with a painful burden that can become professionally paralyzing. For continued mental health, grief needs an outlet.

Find ways of dealing with institutional grief. In one large facility in California, nine children expired in a 14-day period. Yet, no one acknowledged the institutional grief that nearly drowned the personnel. No formal avenues for sharing. Business as usual. Each person was left to struggle alone or to grasp at informal outlets for his mourning. As a result, morale and the healing atmosphere suffered for many months thereafter.

More and more pediatric wards or intensive care units are averting such problems by sponsoring "wakes" when a patient who was widely known and deeply loved finally dies. In an atmosphere of openness and permission, all levels of staff share refreshments, review the patient's life, and ventilate feelings that, if buried, could result in widespread depression and psychosomatic ailments.

Some facilities employ psychiatrists to lead such gatherings. But I believe any nonjudgmental nurse could do as well. I also believe that such "wakes" could well begin before death, when the staff may feel grief most poignantly. After a patient's lingering death, staff members often feel relieved and ready immediately to move past their grief.

Take a break or request a transfer when you approach your emotional limits. Humane supervisors wisely watch and respect the limits of all staff members, trying to keep a troubled nurse from passing the point of personal or permanent harm. Because of guilt and loyalty, though, dedicated pediatric nurses often resist transfers or breaks. Gradually, though, an unduly troubled nurse who refuses a transfer or break will unconsciously take a break from the job — her spirit will put a distance between herself and the trauma she can't handle.

Policies should allow nurses to respect their own limits without undue fuss or embarrassment. Even the strongest nurses should take a break occasionally to preserve their own sense of balance and to serve as models for the less strong. If hospitals honored this policy, nurses who need only a break from work with dying children would take a short leave instead of leaving work permanently.

Unrelenting exposure to dying can produce a kind of eccentricity or obsession. I see manifestation of it among all profes-

Because of guilt and loyalty, dedicated pediatric nurses often resist transfers or breaks. Gradually, though, an unduly troubled nurse who refuses a transfer or break will unconsciously take a break from the job — her spirit will put a distance between herself and the trauma she can't handle.

sionals at death-related conferences and workshops. They tell their gruesome stories to anyone who will listen, morning, afternoon, and far into the night. They need balance. And they can achieve that balance only if they can see death and dying in the wider perspective of life and living.

A gamut of communication

What is the paramount need of a dying child? Pediatric nurses I know unanimously answer, "Communication!" Not only verbal interchange, but the whole gamut of ways humans speak to each other: Conduct, posture, tone, mood . . . drawings, phone calls, games, choice of playmates and toys . . . glances, touches, hugs, teasing, lap-sitting. All send messages.

A dying child's needs come to light most clearly when the delivery team shares its impressions of all forms of communication. But even a nurse who works alone can read the messages quite accurately if she can envision the various ways in which youngsters communicate and can find time to reflect on them. In routine verbal exchanges, you may miss a child's profundity. But when unable or unwilling to talk, he'll resort to a host of conscious or unconscious signals. And the child within you can help break the code to them.

Many of the best known descriptions of dying children would lead us to believe that all dying children pass through common stages and have common needs. This might well be true when we lump all dying children together. But children never die in unison. Each dying is unique. And individual children don't fit so neatly into scholarly pigeonholes. Our communication must focus on discovering the special and distinctive needs of each child.

Certainly generalizations about the needs of dying children can help you understand what to expect from patients. For example, they'll teach you not to be unduly surprised by displaced anger, fear of isolation, depression, hysteria, or bargaining for life with nurses and doctors. You'll learn to expect some youngsters to feel guilty about dying and causing so much trouble. You'll know that even the youngest children sometimes have unfinished business with parents, siblings, or friends. You won't be surprised that some children greet the prospect of death and the end of suffering with relief and acceptance. Above all, you'll renew your appreciation of youngsters' nearly unquenchable spirit of hope.

But no amount of general knowledge can substitute for your

careful assessment of each child. And assessment demands that you listen, watch, and share with others, never letting a particular patient become just another dying child.

Be, as best you can, the kind of person whose presence bespeaks acceptance and nonjudgment. Children arrive at death most peacefully and with their dignity intact if you allow them to confront dying and death in their own way. You may have difficulty identifying the authentic style of a sick child; dying children often adapt their style to the needs of others. But you should try to create an atmosphere in which the child's true self dares to flower.

We all know people whose presence grants us permission to say or be whatever we choose. How different from the normal practices of adults around children! Usually adults act as explainer, protector, caretaker, problem-solver, and final authority. With a dying child, we need to act only as an active and attentive listener, permitting the child's true self to emerge.

If the dying child wishes to talk of sickness and death, let him. If he wishes to pretend, to bargain or to avoid, let him do that too. You shouldn't answer his despair with your own false hopes. But you should keep him talking, maybe asking questions in response to his questions, as is the childlike custom.

If allowed to talk, a child will ultimately discover a far better answer than the vague and often phony assurances we adults usually give. If he won't share by talking, a tender, supportive presence may encourage him to communicate through non-words. Better to allow depression and even despair out in the open, by talking or by providing supportive silence, than to allow a child to suffer alone with only pat and false answers for support.

You can easily enter a child's world, without loss of dignity or propriety, if you respond to him from the child within yourself. So many pediatric nurses excel in this area when others aren't watching. Children don't make speeches, nor do they beat a subject to death by philosophizing at length. They don't find brutally frank answers inappropriate, nor are they baffled by questions as answers. Conversations with children can prosper as long as we don't flash our badge of adulthood.

Pediatric nurses shout in unison that children can spot a phony. And nothing smacks of phoniness more than referring a child who talks about dying to parents or physicians who we know won't answer honestly. Relaying a child's awareness or need to talk to parents or physicians may be necessary. But

We all know people whose presence grants us permission to say or be whatever we choose. How different from the normal practices of adults around children! Usually adults act as explainer, protector, caretaker, problem-solver, and final authority. With a dying child, we need to act only as an active and attentive listener, permitting the child's true self to emerge.

No medical or moral law prevents secrets between nurse and child. You shouldn't push the topic of dying with a child. But if he moves in that direction, maybe toying with the subject or testing your reactions, you certainly can have a confidential discussion without feeling guilty.

pushing a child to do what we know is futile creates a trap that can lead only to disappointment and further frustration.

No medical or moral law prevents secrets between nurse and child. You shouldn't push the topic of dying with a child. But if he moves in that direction, maybe toying with the subject or testing your reactions, you certainly can have a confidential discussion without feeling guilty. After all, you can't reform parents or physicians or expect nonconforming people to measure up suddenly to your expectations. And blaming them for preventing you from talking honestly with the child may be your way of avoiding an onerous task. I find that the children of uncommunicative parents usually deal with the important issues in their young lives by discussing them with playmates, siblings, teachers, fantasy people, anyone other than mom and dad. So, your secret conversations won't usurp the parents' authority.

I'm convinced that nurses must respect a child's confidences. And my conviction grows stronger each time I hear that a Jimmy or a Meredith learned of his diagnosis and prognosis from playmates.

Nowhere in the professional world do I find confidentiality as disrespected as around the dying child. The nurse's family, the neighborhood, the schoolmates, and the entire hospital staff knows everything when the dying child still can only guess. I can't emphasize strongly enough the right of a child to know the name of his illness and something of its seriousness.

However, I believe that the whole question of whether adults should tell children about the seriousness of their illness is declining in importance. Even small children can know about it when they are ready. With television and movies as instructors, they can pick up the announcement from vibrations around the home or hospital.

One of my fondest wishes is that nurses will gain more power and authority in the health care delivery system. But as long as others dominate, you may be able to do no more than pursue their sometimes clumsy course between honesty and confidentiality.

Learn an abiding respect for the maturity that children often gain during lengthy illness. Leukemic children, for example, sometimes display a maturity superior to that of older siblings or even parents. The ups and downs, the disappointments and the many mini-losses they experience prepare them to face dying in a manner nonsufferers can hardly comprehend.

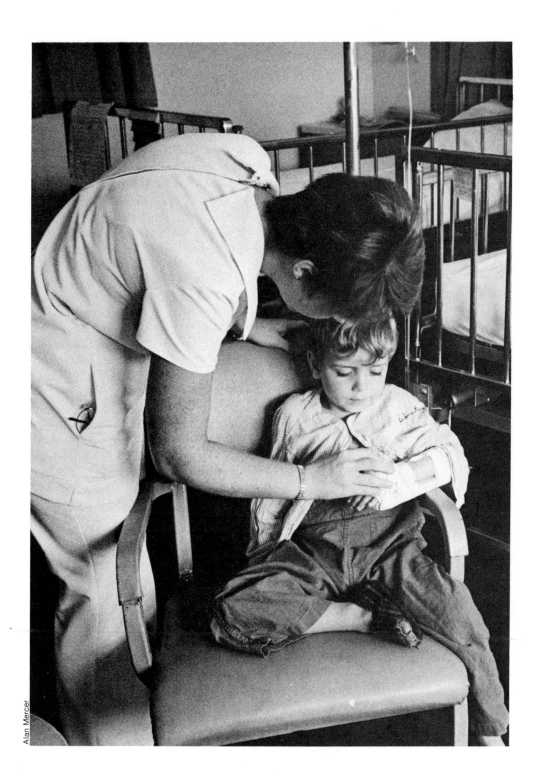

Treating these lingering sufferers as typical children under-estimates their capacity. I have never travelled a path like theirs. Their limitations and pain surpass my experience, as well as the experiences of many pep-talkers and advice-givers the children are sometimes compelled to hear.

Among the cruelest, yet sometimes tempting, ways of deal-ing with dying children is spoiling or bribing them into playing the quiet game. Children pampered through a final illness feel not only lonely, but quite loveless as well. Early, they learned at home to give and to receive love in their family's own way, maybe by teasing, by kidding, by bickering or even by fighting. Now, all that disappears. Instead life becomes filled with presents and constant "yes's."

Nothing seems more calloused in the final days of a young life than to deprive a child of the kind of love that makes life worthwhile. A tired and desperate family cannot always see what is happening. But a freshly involved nurse often can see it at once. You may not be able to preserve the child's life but you can help him and his family to preserve their familial love.

Grief beyond comprehension

Nothing on earth seems to have the permanent impact on parents that an infant's death has. Their grief goes far beyond my comprehension. Usually others can offer nothing more than pity as consolation; only rare individuals can manage their own grief enough to truly help the family.

Often parents internalize their feelings of helplessness and act out those feelings in their social life and marriage. Too often, the death of a baby results in another death — that of the marriage.

When infants die or are dying, you must give careful atten-tion to both parents. The death of a child involves much more than simply his passing. Parents become obsessed with a host of questions about genes, family heritage, parental adequacy: Did they really want the baby? Was it really theirs? Would he have lived with better diet? With earlier detection? Did he die because the mother smoked during pregnancy? Was his death a sign of God's wrath? The litany of possible or imaginary causes grows.

Though grieving yourself, you can become a ready confi-dant to parents during their grief and questioning. Don't regard them as one, but as Mom and Dad, each in need of talking, musing aloud, blaming, questioning, sounding paranoid or foolish, with a minimum of advice or correction. Don't attempt to supply them with easy or final answers. They will find their own final answers, which will enable them to live with themselves and each other. But listen considerately to allow their helplessness to dissipate and a renewed strength to emerge. Remember that when situations defy final answers, important people become as much an answer as the distraught people can find. So you need not play psychiatrist — only a significant someone.

From early on in a fatal illness, remaining sensitive to the varying shades of grief in parents and other family members takes constant self-reminders that families rarely act as a unit in their grief. Often mother's presence at the hospital, while dad works and siblings attend school, results in a whole different grief for her. Sometimes we unwittingly slip into family quarrels by taking sides — casting mom as a sinner and dad as a saint, or pitying one and disdaining the other. A child's death so touches the inner workings of a family that even a Solomon would avoid involvement in family bickerings, offering nothing more than caring and respectful listening. Even if you can't help having your favorites, avoid the futile, defeating practice of entering the fray.

When a child dies suddenly or unexpectedly, relatives need privacy to work through the original shock and disorganization. Generally, hospitals are stingy with space for intimate and profound grief. But you can make do by offering the grief-stricken an acceptance and openness that makes them forget time and place. Touch can be appropriate for some; closeness, for most. Constant verbal assurance will help the family reenter the world of harsh reality from the cocoon of shock. Medication can dissipate the immediacy of the pain and quiet the griever, but human presence — with or without medication — best facilitates normal grieving.

During the grieving process, many people eagerly seek scapegoats on which to vent their anger, particularly if they can't find a rational reason for the death. Hearing nurses defend the quality of their care, their institutions, or the physicians would be comical if it weren't so painful. Allowing the grief-stricken to indict the quality of our care face-to-face requires unusual self-assurance and a special brand of kindness. Remember that blamers seem to feel better after telling someone off, especially people of importance. Your open acceptance of angry tirades can cement a new friendship and

From early on in a fatal illness, remaining sensitive to the varying shades of grief in parents and other family members takes constant self-reminders that families rarely act as a unit in their grief. Sometimes we unwittingly slip into family quarrels by taking sides. A child's death so touches the inner workings of a family that even a Solomon would avoid involvement in family bickerings.

give parents the courage to go beyond their confusion, hurt, and helplessness. Quarrelsome defenses against irrational indictments can lead only to an ongoing spirit of fighting, which stunts the healing process.

After a prolonged dying, family members often finish their grieving before the actual death. They inwardly come to terms with it, are willing to say "goodbye" and prepare for a new tomorrow minus one they love very much. You can sometimes facilitate a discussion of the day when the child will be gone, when only memories and love will remain, if you present an accepting manner. Without words, you can permit parents to see past the death, past their exhaustion, secure in their conviction that they did their best.

When death finally comes, families often feel great relief that all the pain and struggle, all the praying and paying have ended. Many parents can barely admit such a seemingly inappropriate reaction even to themselves, let alone to any but the most understanding nurse. Often, new personnel on the case and friends who have watched the dying from a distance misinterpret acceptance and relief as aloofness or callousness. Guiltily the family may feel obliged to feign sadness and tears for the critics. You can help bewildered parents to avoid that horrible guilt if you let them know that you understand.

Sometimes parents ask nurses to attend the funeral of their child. I've met a few nurses who routinely attend funerals of former patients and many who would never go. Nobody should ever feel guilty about choosing either alternative. We all have special ways of grieving, and your way may or may not include contact outside the hospital.

Working with dying children never will be easy. Each dying will tear away at the core of a nurse who dares to love her patients, touching depths seldom affected by any other human experience. If you dare to love your patients, a part of you will die with each dying child. But in each dying, a new facet of you will be born — the satisfaction of having done some good, a new kind of understanding, a new capacity for loving, and a more profound wisdom about the meaning of life.

A case for prevention

MARGARET O'KEEFE DIRAN

MOST OF YOUR WORK with death and dying will probably focus on helping patients accept impending death. But you may encounter some cases where you'll have to focus on the other extreme: working *against* their acceptance. Those cases, of course, are with suicidal patients.

I'm not talking here about the overtly suicidal patient — the woman who is carried into the emergency room with 20 Seconals in her stomach, or the man who is found by his neighbor barely alive in a gas-filled kitchen.

Nor am I talking primarily about the patient who attempts suicide in the hospital, although this occurs more often than some of us realize.

Instead, I'm talking about the patient on your medical-surgical unit whose suicidal feelings are still hidden from the world, but are very much there, burning like a slow fuse. The populations of our hospital wards are high in such potential suicides, people who have suffered grievous loss: loss of youth, loss of health, loss of body image through mutilating or subtractive surgery, and loss of faith in a life worth living. These patients may be discharged as medically cured, then go home and commit suicide.

I am talking about patients like Carl Smith.

Carl Smith failed to follow his dietary instructions, continued to climb four flights of stairs to his apartment, neglected to take any of his medications, and never returned to see his doctor. His death was attributed to natural causes, but Carl Smith killed himself as surely as if he had held the gun to his head and pulled the trigger. I call this act an "omission suicide."

Carl Smith, 67, lived in a fourth-floor walk-up apartment in the center of the city. He had been retired for a year and a half and widowed for a year. He had a married son and four grandchildren who lived in the suburbs, and whom he saw only on occasional weekends. In January, he was admitted to the hospital suffering from severe chest pain, which was diagnosed as an acute MI. He remained in the hospital for 6 weeks.

Before his discharge, we gave Mr. Smith instructions about his dietary restrictions and his medication. We also asked a social worker to help find him another apartment; we felt four floors up was too much for him. But he flatly refused to move, stating that he had lived there with his wife for more than 30 years, and he "would not know where to go." He said he wanted to "wait for the undertaker in familiar surroundings." He also waved aside our suggestion that he stay with his son until his health improved. "I don't want to be a burden to anyone," he told us.

Several weeks later, he was found dead in his bed. We later learned that he had failed to follow his dietary restrictions, continued to climb four flights of stairs to his apartment, neglected to take any of his medications, and never returned to see his doctor. His death was attributed to natural causes, but Carl Smith killed himself as surely as if he had held a gun to his head and pulled the trigger. I call this act an "omission suicide."

That was some years ago. I have no idea how many such patients I might have successfully intervened with in all my years of nursing. The insights have come to me very slowly. I now feel that a large number of omission suicides are committed every day, all recorded as death by natural causes, and many preventable by skilled and competent nursing intervention. How to know when to intervene? The signs in Carl Smith's case were classic:

He had suffered several severe losses in a brief period: loss of a loved one, loss of work, loss of health, loss of independence.

He felt that he was old.

He was in physical pain.

He was moderately depressed.

He suffered from lack of sleep because of his chest pains at night, and he was fatigued and anxious.

He was a widower.

He withdrew from social contacts.

He had spoken of his feelings of worthlessness and despondency to the nursing staff: "I know you girls work hard, but it's a necessary job you do. It's nice to be needed." "I wish I had your strength."

He had implied that he wished to die. "Enjoy your youth; when you get like me, you're better off dead." "Sometimes I feel I just can't keep this up any longer."

How many Carl Smiths do we encounter in our rounds of the hospital wards? We simply don't know. Statistics show that suicide — overt suicide — ranks as the seventh leading cause of death in the United States, accounting for more than 24,000 deaths per year. Some experts say that many more go undetected, that if all were counted the toll might exceed 100,000 annually. It has been estimated, for example, that as many as 5,000 each year kill themselves in their automobiles, but their deaths are listed as accidental.

A strategic position

Are nurses truly in a position to detect the suicide-prone and intervene to save their lives? The answer is a categorical yes. The position of the nurse is a strategic one. Some studies show that as many as 65% of reported suicide victims had sought medical attention within 3 months before their fatal act, and therefore most likely had been seen by a nurse while the thought of suicide was forming in their minds. Many of these might have been saved if the nurse had been able to identify and help them.

One reason we fail to help the potential suicide is that the idea of self-destruction is repugnant to us. We dismiss the distasteful possibility from our minds as we go about ministering to our sick patients. Perhaps we deny the obvious because it is too threatening for us to acknowledge. To help requires empathy, and empathizing with a potential suicide victim is exhausting and depressing.

We may have a gut reaction to a patient and feel that he is self-destructive, but our dialogue with him merely glosses over the surface and never gets down to the bare fact. We are not open; we are not receptive. He may actually tell us that he wants to die, and we dismiss him with pat answers and platitudes: "Oh, you're not feeling very well now, but you'll feel much better when you get home and back to your own surroundings." Perhaps his hint at feelings of suicide was a call for help, and when he hears platitudes in return, he withdraws.

Far better for us to face it squarely: "You talked about dying yesterday. Would you like to explain what you mean by that?" We might draw some of his grieving process out into the open. This can be one of the most valuable parts of our nursing care. We must learn to give of ourselves, to try to understand what it is the patient is trying to tell us. Pat answers are really our way of defending ourselves from possible involvement with the patient. The potential suicide will give out the hints necessary for us to recognize him, if only we ask for them.

How to spot the potential suicide

The first step in the battle is to identify the high-risk patient. Some of the questions to ask yourself in assessing the degree of risk in a given patient are listed in Table 1.

If Carl Smith had been asked these questions, he would have answered *yes* to six of them. I believe that a patient who answers *yes* to three or more should be followed up with careful observation, interviews, and, depending on the information gleaned, possibly a psychiatric consult. Throughout your nursing intervention, keep the following in mind.

It is not easy to ask a patient, "Have you ever entertained the idea of killing yourself?" Perhaps you feel you could not handle the situation if he answers *yes*. If so, you need to work

TABLE 1 — Suicide Evaluation Sheet

Every "yes" answer increases the possibility of suicide.

1. Has the patient sustained a recent loss (of job, friend, money, loved one, home, status, or part of the body by subtractive surgery)? Include miscarriage or postpartum state. ☐ YES ☐ NO
2. Is he isolated from others socially, without friends? ☐ YES ☐ NO
3. Has he ever attempted suicide? ☐ YES ☐ NO
4. Has a member of his family ever attempted suicide? ☐ YES ☐ NO
5. Has he ever been treated for mental illness? ☐ YES ☐ NO
6. Is he old, bereaved, or in physical pain? ☐ YES ☐ NO
7. Does he view suicide as a release? ☐ YES ☐ NO
8. Is he diagnosed as a psychotic? ☐ YES ☐ NO
9. If so, does he hear voices telling him to kill himself? ☐ YES ☐ NO
10. Is he depressed? ☐ YES ☐ NO
11. Has he said he wished to die, or has he failed to perform life-saving acts (refused to give himself insulin, or refused to take digitalis or other medical treatment, or said he cannot irrigate his colostomy or has "no need to learn")? ☐ YES ☐ NO
12. Does he have a history of self-destructive behavior (consistently reckless, accident-prone, addicted to alcohol or other drugs, given to self-mutilation)? ☐ YES ☐ NO
13. Does he lack a religious background that enjoins against suicide? ☐ YES ☐ NO

HOW MUCH DO YOU KNOW ABOUT SUICIDE?

Your understanding of suicide is your first line of defense against it. Check yourself out by answering *true* or *false* to these statements:
1. Suicide accounts for very few deaths annually in the United States.
2. Suicide is most common in those who are hopelessly ill and can no longer cope with a terminal diagnosis.
3. The age group in which most suicides occur is 25 to 40 years.
4. The incidence of suicide among physicians is double to triple that in the general population.
5. Suicide is more common among the lower socioeconomic groups. Laborers and blue-collar workers are more prone to commit suicide than the professional person.
6. Repeated statements such as "I would be better off dead" from a patient should be taken seriously.
7. Suicide rates are higher in cities than in rural areas.
8. The incidence of suicide among unwed mothers is high.
9. The presence of a psychosis increases the likelihood of suicide.
10. Alcoholism and drug addiction are rarely responsible for a suicidal act.

ANSWERS

1. *False.* Suicide ranks as the seventh leading cause of death in the United States. It accounts for more than 24,000 deaths annually.
2. *False.* Terminally ill patients commit suicide less often than patients with chronic illness, who have a suicide rate higher than average.
3. *False.* Persons 60 years of age or older constitute the age group most likely to commit suicide.
4. *True.* Physicians have a much higher incidence of suicide than the lay population.
5. *False.* There appears to be a direct relationship between social status and suicide. The higher one is on the socioeconomic scale, the more susceptible he is to suicide.
6. *True.* Some 60% to 80% of those who commit suicide communicate their intent beforehand.
7. *True.* The more intimately one is involved with others, the lower the probability of suicide. The person isolated in a city apartment who doesn't know his neighbor is far more prone to suicide than his country cousin.
8. *False.* A recent study in Michigan shows that suicide among pregnant women is very rare.
9. *True.* A psychotic person who is impulsive, suspicious, inappropriately fearful, and subject to panic states is a potential suicide candidate. The risk is greatly increased if, in addition, the patient hears voices commanding him to kill himself.
10. *False.* Weakening of higher cerebrocortical functions by sleeplessness, barbiturates, alcohol, or other drugs strongly contributes to the potential for self-destruction. Under the influence of alcohol or drugs, the death wish grows and judgment is clouded.

11. A person with a history of suicide committed by a close family member is a higher suicide risk.
12. Suicide is more prevalent among the divorced and widowed than among the married.
13. Black Americans are more suicide-prone than whites.
14. Suicide ranks as a leading cause of death among college students.
15. Depression is the most common precursor of suicide.
16. There is no relationship between recent childbirth or surgery and suicide.
17. A person with a history of a previous suicide attempt is more likely to commit suicide.
18. Suicidal persons rarely seek medical attention, so it is difficult for a community-based or hospital nurse to identify them.
19. When interviewing a patient who has a high potential for suicide, never question him directly about his self-destructive ideas. Doing so may strengthen the suggestion of suicide in his mind and prompt him to make the attempt.
20. Most suicides in the United States are committed with a drug overdose.

Scoring

Now add up your score.
Give yourself five points
for every correct answer.
100-90 Good
90-80 Fair
Below 80 Poor

---

11. *True.* Suicide by a close family member increases one's potential to do the same. Identification is thought to be a factor. Such suicides can occur as an "anniversary phenomenon," the attempt being made on a birthday or anniversary of the relative's death.
12. *True.* Suicide is more common among the divorced and widowed.
13. *False.* Black Americans presently have a lower incidence of suicide than do whites but the incidence of suicide among blacks has been steadily rising over the past decade.
14. *True.* Suicide ranks as the second leading cause of death, after accidents, among college students.
15. *True.* Depression is the most common emotional experience of the suicidal candidate. Guilt, especially over a dead relative; feelings of worthlessness; intense wish for punishment; withdrawal and hopelessness; and anxiety and agitation are all high-risk emotions.
16. *False.* The incidence of suicide rises after childbirth or surgery. Loss of status is thought to be a factor in postpartum suicide. Subtractive or mutilative surgery is a threat to body image.
17. *True.* Over 50% of those who commit suicide have a history of a previous attempt. When interviewing these patients, you should determine the setting of the initial attempt. Was it done when he was alone? Was he found by accident? This information is helpful in assessing the strength of the death wish.
18. *False.* More than 65% of all suicide victims seek medical attention within three months before the suicide. A careful interviewer should be able to identify the high-risk patient.
19. *False.* If a patient does not discuss this with you, bring it up yourself. Repeated studies have shown that open discussion has never harmed anyone, and it has helped many.
20. *False.* Each year firearms account for about 12,000 suicides, making gunshot wounds the leading cause of death among suicide victims.

to put the idea of suicide in perspective in your own mind. It can be prevented, but only if you face your responsibility to get the facts from the patient and to bring those facts before the attending physician if you feel it necessary.

Don't feel that your open discussion of these matters with the patient might increase the possibility of his committing suicide. Quite the opposite is the case. He sees life as subject to intolerable constraints. Talking about it is therapeutic, cathartic: he can be led to understand that these problems can be worked through, and that he has the strength and resources to do so.

You're not alone in this effort. You can draw on family, friends, neighbors, and community resources, as well as physicians, psychiatrists, psychologists, social workers, and appropriate guidance counselors.

How to intervene   Once you believe you have identified a potential suicide, discuss the patient with the attending physician and suggest that a plan of care be initiated. The physician may wish to request consultation with a psychiatrist. Carefully document statements made to the staff by the patient that give a clue to his mental state. Then plan an interview with the patient to explore his ideas about suicide in depth. Set aside time from your daily schedule and conduct the interview in a quiet, comfortable place where there will be few interruptions. You might ask such questions as these:

1. You said yesterday that you would be better off dead. Why do you feel this way?

2. Have you ever thought about taking your own life?

3. What plans, if any, have you made concerning this action?

4. Do you feel that taking your own life would hurt anyone else? Why?

5. What religious beliefs do you have concerning suicide? (You should not assume that the profession of any particular religion will prevent suicide. If the act of suicide violates the patient's religious beliefs, however, you have found a tool with which to work. You should then consult a clergyman.)

6. Have you ever had ideas like this at any other time in your life?

7. Do you believe that these feelings could pass away if you were given help?

8. What help would you choose if it were available?

This type of questioning will show the patient that you care about him and that you are acknowledging his calls for help. It also helps him to understand that his feelings are not so unusual, given the circumstances. He is not unique, not alone. Sharing his thoughts with others frequently decreases the intensity of his feelings. You may find after the interview that the patient will manifest a surprising decrease of anxiety. He might even say, "I feel a great relief; I've never talked to anyone about these feelings before."

Record the results of your interview. Write down the answers to such questions as:

1. How long has the patient had these thoughts?

2. What does he feel the cause to be? How much insight does he appear to have?

3. Has he ever had these feelings at any other time in his life? If so, what prompted them? How long did they last? What occurred to stop them, if anything?

4. What method of suicide has he contemplated? If medication, where did he plan to get it? If he plans to use a gun, does he own one or know where one is available? If he plans to use an automobile, where and under what circumstances? (If he is unclear as to the details, note that.)

5. What is motivating him to stay alive? What does he cherish and hold dear to him? What type of help or change in his life would deter him from suicide?

On your nursing care plan, list all *positive* information you get from the patient. This is information you can use to begin your plan of care at once. Begin with the feelings of doubt about the wisdom of suicide that already exist in the patient's mind. Bolster those doubts by positive reinforcement. Draw out and use the patient's strengths. You can build upon his reasons for remaining alive and weaken his reasons for contemplating suicide. You might prepare a chart such as the one shown in Table 2 on the next page.

Remember to avoid holding out false promises or minimizing the patient's problem. This may serve temporarily to lift his mood, but he will soon realize the implausibility of what you say, and this will further intensify his depression, reduce his trust in you, and build a wall between you that will be difficult to penetrate.

If you conduct the interview, be sure to continue seeing the patient on a one-to-one basis, and share what you learn with

Don't feel that your open discussion of the patient's personal problems might increase the possibility of his committing suicide. Quite the opposite is the case. He sees life as subject to intolerable constraints. Talking about it is therapeutic, cathartic: he can be led to understand that these problems can be worked through.

the other team members, who will help you to evaluate progress. How do you measure progress? First, by the patient's increasing ability to express the losses he has sustained, and his willingness to listen to alternatives to suicide. He might tell you that he is relieved to know that he has alternatives. He might say that he had a time limit for suicide, but that it doesn't seem that imperative now. Maybe he'll do it later if things don't work out.

TABLE 2 — Assessing the Suicidal Patient

Assessment	Possible Approach
POSITIVE: Loves his sons; does not wish to bring disgrace upon them.	Loving others is a beautiful part of life. Taking his own life will upset his children and their children and bring them guilt. He is fortunate to have sons he loves.
Catholic. Feels that if he committs suicide his church will refuse him the sacraments.	Consult a priest (if possible one that knows him). Ask the priest to visit him. Tell the patient that his religious beliefs can help him now.
States that he would not wish to die if he could be of some use to someone else.	Discuss options for service open to him. Volunteer work; religious and charity work.
NEGATIVE: Considers his physical strength gone. Seems unable to accept the change in status that accompanies this loss.	Offer him alternatives to physical strength. Discuss volunteer work such as reading to blind patients. Explain that his physical condition will improve with time and that his mental attitude is a strong influence.
Has found life very difficult since the death of his wife.	Explain the grief process to him. Encourage him to discuss his loss. Direct him to new interests. Contact local senior citizen group and ask that a member visit.
Is depressed and has been for some time.	Depression is a natural consequence of the losses he has suffered. Time, verbalization, and medication can do a great deal to reduce the intensity of the emotion he is feeling.

Before the patient is discharged, discuss his case with the community-based nurse. Advise the patient to get in touch with his physician if suicidal ideas return. Suggest to the physician that he notify the nearest community mental health center and refer the patient there for possible evaluation and group therapy.

Before discharge

Instruct the patient to:

1. Avoid drinking alcohol, taking sedatives, and becoming overtired. Any one of these can intensify suicidal ideas.

2. Take medication for depression regularly as recommended by his physician. Do not omit or alter dosages.

3. Keep handy the address and telephone number of the local suicide prevention center, and call them if suicidal feelings become overwhelming.

4. Remember that suicide is most often an impulsive act committed at the height of emotional stress. He should fight the impulse with all available resources. Sometimes it is best just to go to bed and sleep. Poor impulse control often is the result of fatigue.

Finally, what of the overtly suicidal patient, the one who was admitted following an unsuccessful suicide attempt? In all likelihood he will be admitted to a psychiatric ward, but whether he is or not, there is only one difference in your nursing care. The first, and often the most difficult, step has already been taken: he is identified.

SKILLCHECK 1

All of the preceding chapters paint a clear picture of how experts work with dying patients. But will you be able to incorporate their experiences into your own practice?

To help you answer that question, here are seven hypothetical situations that you may encounter with dying patients. After reading the question following each "test case," write down as many plausible answers as you can imagine. Although we've listed only a few in the "Answers" section (page 185), we suggest you write as many as possible to stimulate your assessment skills and your ability to see each situation from several perspectives. In real life situations, of course, you would then test out each possibility through conversations with the patient. Only in that way could you decide which is the real explanation for his particular behavior.

1. Tuesday, the doctor told Helen, a young divorced mother of two, that she has terminal cancer. But as you're helping her with her morning care on Thursday, she says, "I've been so worried about my little girls. But I'll be well enough to go home and take care of them in a few months."

What are some likely explanations for her comment?

2. For three weeks you've been caring for Don, a 35-year-old who is terminally ill. Since you first met him, he has been angry, hostile, and difficult to cope with. In the past week, though, as he has moved closer to death, he has become very quiet. When you care for him, he hardly seems to notice your presence.

What are some likely explanations for his change in behavior?

3. Maggie, who has terminal cancer, is about your age. While caring for her, you've tried to make casual conversation but she responds with only one-word or two-word answers. When you finally ask if she saw the championship tennis match on television yesterday, she snaps, "I spend most of my time reading. But I don't suppose *you* can understand that. You're probably too busy to ever pick up a book."

What are some likely explanations for her comment?

4. Louise, a 45-year-old woman with inoperable cancer of the colon, tells you about a friend who had cancer of the colon two years ago. "But you know," she says, "she's leading a perfectly normal life today."

What might her comment indicate?

5. For several weeks, John has been obsessed with thoughts of his terminal illness, fluctuating between a desperate hope that he'll overcome it and utter depression. But now he suddenly announces that he plans to will his body to a local medical school and his eyes to an eye bank. You notice, too, that for the first time he has a Bible by his bed.

What are some possible explanations for his new behavior?

6. For a week, 82-year-old Mr. Jennings has talked anxiously about his grandson's wedding. Now he promises you that, if you'll help convince his doctor to let him go to it, he'll "never ask you for anything else."

What are some logical interpretations of his comment?

7. As a student nurse, you've just been assigned to Mrs. Graham, a terminally-ill patient who has a daughter about your age. When you enter her room for the first time, she says, "You *will not* take care of me. I don't want a student. I want a *nurse* who knows what she's doing."

How would you interpret her comment?

For the next situation, write a brief essay exploring your reactions. The "Answers" section doesn't provide a "correct" essay, but it does list some questions to help you evaluate your response and the attitudes it reflects.

8. As a nurse on a busy general medical-surgical unit, you are delivering evening medications to patients. As you walk into the first room, the cardiac patient sitting in the corner looks at you anxiously and says, "Nurse, I think I'm going to die tonight."

Write a few paragraphs explaining your feelings and how you would respond to the patient.

Dealing
with the
family

Confronting expected death

EILEEN RINEAR

MUCH HAS BEEN said and written lately about the needs of the dying. Much less has been written and said about the needs of survivors who must begin to live with their loss. What is happening to a patient's family when they know that death is waiting outside the door?

I remember one Easter Sunday when a family was gathered alongside the figure of their husband and father. He'd been such a healthy, happy, full-of-life person. Now, he lay dying of a terminal illness. His half-grown sons stood beside him, drawn, awkward, and mute. His wife stared at his closed lids in sad disbelief. A young nurse, standing by, started to leave. That's tactful, she thought. Give them the privacy they need for what must be these last moments. But as she moved away from the bed, the wife caught her gaze. "Please —'' she said. The nurse lingered.

For what? To help the patient? Everything she could do had been done for him. To talk to the family? What could she say? To get the doctor? Get the chaplain? Say a prayer? How could she begin to meet their awful need? She wished she were at the other end of the hospital.

Impulsively, the nurse put her hand out and gripped the woman's shoulder. She was surprised at how much comfort seemed to come from the gesture for both of them. After a moment, she said, "I wish I'd known him. Tell me what kind of man he is." The dam broke as they all began to talk at once.

We can do a great deal to make death more bearable not only for those who must meet it, but also for the grieving witnesses. As in this instance, I have seen us do it. We can influence at the outset the way a family will begin coping with their loss, their grief, their inevitable guilt. And since we can do it, we have the most urgent obligation to see that it is done. No more conspiracies of polite evasion. No more holding back for the next fellow to do it — or for the next patient, the next crisis: these people who are bereft have need and crisis enough. And insofar as you help them, you help your own patient until he has breathed his last. How do we know the father dying on Easter Day didn't find comfort in his family's voices as they all tried at once to tell of him and what he meant to them?

First of all, listen

The ability to assess, understand, and empathize is not necessarily innate. Much of it has to be cultivated. I've found the best way to learn is to listen.

Listen to what, you say? Most people will readily give you clues as to what they want to discuss. Or, to get things started, you may have to ask a question — not necessarily such an impulsive one as the young nurse did in her experience, but at any rate a sympathetic one. And if they ask you a question instead, rather than giving them an answer that will shut them up, keep up a therapeutic flow with another gentle question.

Two nurses, for example, were trying to comfort the daughter of an elderly man who was critically ill and probably going to die. "I'm so afraid he won't get well," the daughter confided. "Well, we all have to die some time," the first nurse was about to say. And though she would have meant it compassionately, it still would have come as a blow; the woman didn't really want her fears confirmed, not so abruptly.

But the second nurse said very quietly, "Supposing he didn't get well?" And then the daughter was free to talk about her feelings with someone willing to listen and help.

Of course, supporting a relative or a family through an illness and a death is not the same as providing answers for all their questions or solutions for all their problems. But it can help them just to maintain contact with someone, a contact that is honest and undeceiving. Listening offers direct comfort and support. Listening is an invaluable tool for you, too, in planning an individualized approach to caring for the patient and his family, an approach that gives realistic help and is based on realistic goals for them.

And there's another thing about listening. Nonverbal communication is usually a more reliable index to an individual's emotional status than words are. The young wife's unspoken plea on Easter not to leave them, the hundred meanings you notice all around you where words say one thing — nothing at all — and the unguarded look or gesture says quite another, these can tell you worlds. Responding to unspoken cues rather than stiff phrases may be the key you need to open the door between you and the reluctant family.

Today the hospital's enlightened eagerness to treat the patient, not merely the disease, includes a willingness to help the family as well. This help takes supportive and psychological forms. But we nurses have trouble in learning and teaching, let alone in using any real skill in the interactive process of communication. Is this because our education places so much emphasis on *doing* things?

Some nurses tell me they feel awkward and uneasy if, rather than performing a tangible task, they are simply listening. They feel downright guilty if they are sitting and talking with a patient or his family when the head nurse or supervisor comes along. And this can be further complicated when the issue under discussion is one they feel is emotionally charged, difficult, or inappropriate.

But remember, just admitting a person to the hospital doesn't lessen his and his family's need for communication, contact, and security; if anything, these needs are intensified in such impersonal surroundings. We must recognize this. We mustn't be so easily intimidated by the hospital's functional operation that we lose sight of priorities. *We must never see needed communication as conflicting with visible physical care*. It is easily worth just as much—and the enlightened hospital staff or supervisor would be the first to tell you so.

As for those awkward, difficult, or emotionally charged conversations, try changing roles with your confidant. Put yourself in his place, not to show you what you would want if someone you loved was dying, but to help you be more receptive to just what that family needs. You won't automatically get to know what is right for them. But your intervention will at least be based then on what they need in contrast to what you

Nonverbal communication is usually a more reliable index to an individual's emotional status that words are. The hundred meanings you notice all around you where words say one thing — nothing at all — and the unguarded look or gesture says quite another, these can tell you worlds. Responding to unspoken cues rather than stiff phrases may be the key you need to open the door between you and the reluctant family.

believe you would be seeking in their place. To be most effective, your communication should take into account not only your own personal style but the family's personal history and background.

No two family units and no two individuals are alike. There is no stereotype for grief. The family itself and each of its members will be differently affected by death, depending upon their own personalities, their relationship to the dying person, his age, their previous experience with death, and their cultural and religious tradition.

The best listener also knows

To understand a family and its belief and concept of death, use every means to gather as much data as you can so you will know them *as individuals*. Obviously this can take a good deal of time. Yet this expenditure of time — most valuable when undertaken early rather than late in the course of the patient's disease — is a critical step in establishing trust and rapport. Both lay the framework for a deep and stable relationship.

In the interim between diagnosis and death, you will need these relationships and this communication. They are very supportive for the family who must begin to acknowledge the loss it faces. They are an ease for the family plagued with guilt because of wishes or thoughts that are deemed unacceptable (no matter how common). And they will help provide certainty for those who are perplexed by treatments for the disease and bewildered by its uncertain course.

Shared care

Give the family members a role in the care of a terminally ill loved one. This is especially helpful when they express a desire to do something, or say they feel helpless just sitting around. Let them feed him, give him his bath, help with mouth care, or rub his back. These duties not only help the hospital staff in general, the busy staff nurses, and probably the patient. They also help the family. For many families admit that, although they can accept the fact that death is imminent, the suffering it may entail is too much for them to face.

Such comforting tasks as these partly relieve their anxiety. They lessen their feelings of regret and guilt, too, when death does come. For there is surely no death in which the survivor does not, for one thing, in some small corner of himself say, "Thank God it wasn't me; I'm still alive." And feel guilty.

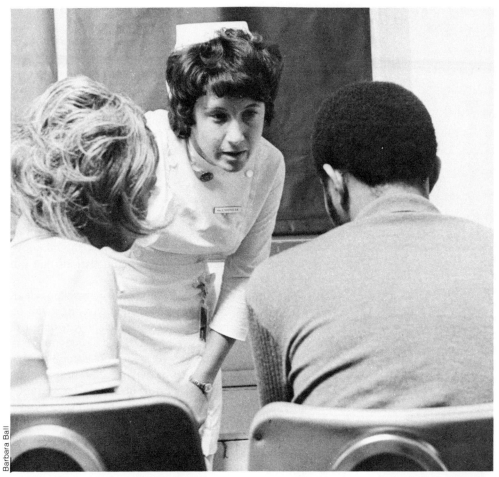

You should assure the family that any measures the patient needs for relief of pain and promotion of physical comfort will be used. Give them all the information you can about his care and comfort. And never quite shut the door on the possibility of hope, either.

We hope that society may one day mature enough to come to grips with the issue of unnecessary pain. Then it can take gut-level, definitive action to relieve the legal pressures on physicians that so often keep them from prescribing adequate sedation, no matter how large compared to what is normally given. Meantime, though, no one will be callously left to suffer unaided.

When death seems imminent, I believe the family should be called to the bedside, if they are not already there. Oftentimes, I've noticed that the hospital staff is reluctant to do this: they

To understand a family and its belief and concept of death, use every means to gather as much data as you can so you will know them as individuals. This expenditure of time — most valuable when undertaken early rather than late in the course of the patient's disease — is a critical step in establishing trust and rapport.

don't want to bring bad news; they fear their estimation of the timing will be inaccurate.

True, no one can predict death's time clock. Still, if there is any doubt, summon the family anyway. The overall risk associated with calling them early or too often is considerably less than that of keeping them uninformed.

If you can't watch for the family when they come, designate someone in the right place to keep watch for them and to alert you and the rest of the staff. Upon arrival, they should be directed to some private place where the doctor can talk with them: he can answer their questions, he can tell them of pertinent developments in the patient's condition. You should be there if you can, not only to act as a familiar support but to learn exactly what the physician is saying. You should know this to guide you later in answering related questions that the family may ask.

If, in talking to the doctor, the family gets answers not clear to them, or answers that seem to be entangled in a web of professional jargon, they must be given clear translations. Families have a right not only to be heard and to question, but to understand. We must be sure they are not forced to shy away from us — or from the truth they need — because we appear busy, annoyed, overpowerful, or merely indifferent.

Sometimes the smallest act will suffice to win their confidence, so long as it reflects kindness and concern. I recall the family of an Italian grandmother dying of cancer, all of them obviously close to her and fond of her. One day they were scattered about the hall near her room because some personal function — perhaps her catheter — had to be tended to. A nurse with whom they had previously formed a bond came upon the disconsolate group in the hall. When she invited them into a nearby lounge to have some tea with her, she established a rapport with them that they relied upon in later exchange. Some similar kindness can likewise win the trust of a family you have not previously met. So long as you really want to help, your feeling will surely come through.

Once the family is gathered, it should be given the opportunity to spend some time alone with the patient. This chance for intimacy should not be displaced by any well-meaning nurse or other staff member who smothers the patient with care, effectively blocking out any bystanders. If you are the nurse on duty and you have assessed the patient's status, check with the family from time to time to see if they need anything. This conveys your thoughtfulness and concern. But it doesn't make them feel either supervised or excluded.

When death is imminent

This is one time when you should be wary about how whatever you say and do to the patient will be perceived. We presume that you are not in the habit of agitating either the patient or his family. Nonetheless, remember that families in times of stress are supersensitive. They notice far more of what is taking place around them than they ordinarily would. They see the decor in detail. They notice the smallest part of an attitude toward their beloved patient or themselves. In this intense and critical period, be sure that your respect for the dignity of your patient's life is clearly evident.

Sometimes these patients are in coma. I always talk to comatose patients as I would to someone fully conscious. I tell them what I am going to do before I do it, whether it's turning them in bed, giving an injection, or inserting an oxygen catheter. Respecting their dignity in this way not only helps the family to know that I do so; it helps me to continue to care for that person as a *person*. Otherwise you can begin to feel you are merely confronted with 150 pounds of flesh, organ systems, tubes, and drainage apparatuses.

I encourage families also to talk to the comatose patient. As for the patient, we're not sure that he can hear us or understand us. But we can never be sure that he cannot. When you recall the rare situation where a patient thought to be unresponsive later regained consciousness only to relate to others all that had been said over him as he supposedly lay unconscious, it is too costly a risk to take. Obviously, you cannot condone indiscriminate bedside comments about the patient, his personality, his disease, his extensive care and the time it takes, his prognosis, or anything else of the sort.

And as for the family, you'd be surprised how much relief they can gain from this, especially if they have gotten to the hospital after the patient has lost consciousness. When you tell them he may still be able to hear them even if he can't indicate it, this will give them hope there is still a link for communion with him.

We must also take the family into consideration when doing some kind of procedure in their presence. This is especially true in a coronary or intensive care unit when close relatives are allowed restricted visiting privileges. Though this isn't a

If the family's intensity of emotion is less than you were prepared for, avoid making judgments. Grief and its direct expression are not always closely correlated. And if you do feel judgmental toward them, it will be almost sure to come through in nonverbal ways. The family is already having to contend with loss — even if in its own way. Your disapproval surely won't help them.

common setting for "expected death," and although here "extraordinary life-saving and life-maintaining measures" do take place, still death does threaten.

Yet all too often, the families of patients in these units are not prepared by the staff for what to expect. This results in unnecessary anxiety and stress, and they find themselves overwhelmed. We must never turn from sentient human beings into automatons so immersed in our tasks and duties that we forget all appearances. What is routine life-saving equipment to us may be an unholy array to the family waiting in the background. We must never use a wall of machines to isolate the patient, family, and nurse from one another.

All we have to do is take a few minutes to explain things to the family so as to prepare them for what they will see. This will make it easier for them, for the patient, and for us.

Ideally, the patient's own physician should be there when he dies. But it can't always happen that way, of course. If you yourself have the job of notifying the family, take great care to convey empathy and respect. Again, they need a quiet, private place to express their grief, and to collect their thoughts. You should stay with them.

And yet, if their seeming relation with the deceased turns out not to be what you expected, if their intensity of emotion is less than you were prepared for, avoid making judgments. Grief and its direct expression are not always closely correlated. And if you do feel judgmental toward them, it will be almost sure to come through in nonverbal ways. The family is already having to contend with loss — even if in its own way. Your disapproval surely won't help them. Besides, it's just possible that you would be passing along some of your own anger, frustration, or depression in having lost this patient.

Once death has come, the focus belongs on the surviving family, and on anything that can strengthen them and make this experience more bearable for them. This will cut down their later load of regret and guilt. Acknowledge the things they did to make life easier and more meaningful for the member now dead. Pray with them, if it is compatible with their religious beliefs. Doris A. Howell, MD, pediatric hematologist, believes that people are more receptive to whatever you say to help them when it is worded into a prayer.

Touch can be used as a means of emotional expression and an agent of comfort. This age-old form of communication and feeling transcends verbal limitations and human boundaries.

And the final kindnesses — simply spending time with them, offering a cup of coffee, obtaining a sedative if needed, or just making a phone call for them — will make all the difference as to how they remember this situation and begin to cope with it.

Dr. Howell has also observed that a family will vividly recall the events surrounding a death. They may relive this original experience, she thinks, when they are confronted with illness or death in the future. This is especially true when they have witnessed the agonizing death of someone they love. A very alert young funeral director put it another way. "In our profession we are not concerned with time or the saving of a life," she says. "Death has already occurred. What we are leaving is impressions."

And your own feelings? Why should you hide them, so long as you continue to do your work? As Dr. Howell has said, "This does not mean not to cry. You have a right to demonstrate whatever emotion you are feeling as long as it doesn't interfere with what has to be done . . . the expression of emotion at the death of a person is nothing to be ashamed of. Is there any better way of letting a family know how much you cared about their loved one?"

The hospital will have become so much a part of some families' lives through this encounter with death that it may be very difficult for them to separate from it altogether, especially if they find no fault with the care it gave. Certainly these families should be followed up later when the work of grief has begun.

I remember one young couple who had lost their firstborn, then 5, to neuroblastoma after a long and painful siege. The father's grief seemed normal and direct enough, but the mother did not seem to feel the loss appropriately. It was as if she were still living in a kind of stunned hope that the verdict could be reversed.

My greatest concern is for these people who feel death's impact at a much later time than most people — for feel it they do. They are likely to receive the least support when they need it most. Where everybody besieges a family with the desire to help just after a death has occurred, their concern can be short-lived. The survivors are soon expected to get over it and get on with the business of living. Now even normal grief is a fairly lengthy process, and grief can be markedly prolonged by such feelings as unresolved guilt or strong ambivalence toward the one now dead.

We telephoned this particular mother 2 weeks after the funeral to learn how she was and to offer any help or social services we might be able to get for her. When she refused these offers calmly, we told her that we would call her again in a few months to keep in touch. To our surprise, though, she came back with her husband for a visit in another 3 weeks, explaining somewhat shamefacedly that she just couldn't get over feeling that something of her baby remained within the hospital walls. At least by now she seemed to have begun to feel her loss, which meant to us that she could eventually begin to recover. The day she saw us, she confessed at last that she had always felt guilty toward the dead child because she hadn't originally wanted it. We were able to help her with her negative feelings. But if at death we had closed the hospital door to her, one wonders how long this mother's proper work of mourning would have been inhibited.

At a time when the well of everybody else's understanding has dried up and all the sympathetic ears have gone deaf, an open line of communication with health professionals can sometimes be even more helpful than in the period right after death. There's no point in attending a patient's funeral, as I have known some nurses to do, if you are never going to see the family after the service.

Sometimes hospital therapy groups can be started to help the bereaved. Certain lay organizations composed of people who have experienced a like situation can also help.

Besides losing patients, one other thing can temper our own feelings about bereavement and family after-care. That's a personal brush with death. If we have a grave illness, or if we lose someone dear to us, we will develop an even greater awareness of how it feels to be on the "other" side. This experience is almost sure to come sooner or later to all who live long enough, and we nurses will be no exception.

In an impersonal society of numbers and masses, we must still find time for the individual. We must allow ourselves to touch and experience some measure of another's pain or loss. We must comfort him and empathize with him. We must let him know he is not alone: we have chosen to share this experience with him.

I saw a sign in a bookshop window the other day. It read, "Let's build bridges, not walls." It is my fervent hope that we can learn to do this not only with the dying but with the still-living as well.

Stages in bereavement

JANE C. WILLIAMS

INVOLVEMENT WITH FAMILIES of the dying certainly isn't safe, secure work. But we have no right to call ourselves helping persons if we don't dare take that risk of deep personal involvement. We may make mistakes. But, to paraphrase an old saying, it's better to try and to make mistakes than never to try at all.

One way to avoid mistakes, though, is to realize that families of the dying, like the patients themselves, often go through stages of grief: denial, anger, bargaining, depression, acceptance. We must learn to recognize these stages so we can help families through them. And we must be careful not to fall prey to them ourselves.

I learned this lesson with the family of one patient. John was 24 when he was burned over 70% of his body. I knew, as did everyone else on the medical team, what minimal chance of survival he had. Yet none of us wanted to believe anything other than that he would win his struggle for life.

With each passing day, we all seemed more secure in our denial of his critical condition. His young wife returned to their home upstate, and went back to work. His parents left for their home 2,000 miles away just before the end of the 3-week critical period. I talked with his parents about staying. My gut reaction was to tell them to stay, but I didn't. I felt they'd gone through enough and should go back to the rest of their family, and that he would surely survive. Three days after they left, he died.

As professionals, we have to be extremely conscious of our own feelings getting in the way. Denial is a normal part of the grieving process, something that's easier to recognize in others than in yourself. And yet we *must* recognize it in ourselves if we're to continue functioning in helpful ways. But with John, denial of the family and staff just fed into each other. There wasn't one of us who could rise above it and face the painful fact that this young man was probably not going to survive. The one who suffered most, of course, was John, who died without the support of those dearest to him. The guilt his family felt was devastating. Nor has my own guilt been absolved, though I have learned an invaluable lesson.

Sometimes, however, the denial you come up against is so great that it can seem impossible to break through. False hopes are offered up, untrue stories are told, and tremendous amounts of energy are consumed in keeping denial alive. Indeed, many staff members are relieved when a patient's family maintains denial; then they are not forced into dealing with their own discomfort and fear of death. But when the family's defenses crumble before the reality of it all, the fall is very great. Sometimes, the family will try to cling to denial even after death. And unless this is handled properly, the healing process of grieving can never truly begin.

Take the case of a woman in her 50s whom I'll call Mrs. O. Her husband, like the young man John, was the victim of a tragic accident that turned him into a human torch. He died 2 weeks later, conscious to the end.

During this time, Mrs. O. created quite a disturbance on the nursing unit. She was extremely concerned about getting an insurance form signed, and would insult and pester the nurses and other members of the staff about it. When I discussed this with the head nurse, I told her it seemed that Mrs. O. was unable to cope with her critically ill husband, was not hearing the doctors who were telling her how sick he was, and that her anger, her emphasis on the insurance form, had to be understood in the terms of denial and shock. This helped make the staff more tolerant of her.

The staff, however, was so intensely occupied with trying to save Mr. O.'s life that they failed to give either him or his wife as much emotional support as they could have. Later, the staff's apparent frustration at failing to save his life showed up in another way. When I tried to discuss the case with them, I would get curt answers and obvious signs of uneasiness. In fact, though this particular staff will often discuss discharged patients, they won't even mention those who die.

Mrs. O.'s first conversation with me when her husband was still alive consisted of her telling me this: her husband was very ill and she found she had trouble adjusting to his absence until he could come home. Her first conversation with me *after* his death conveyed her feelings of shock, anger, denial. She blamed the doctors for not telling her how sick he was. Yet she said it with the same lack of affect as before the death. It was as though she still couldn't accept the reality of it.

I visited her 2 weeks later. This time she only wanted to reminisce — about the accident, the horrible hospitalization, his suffering, and a painful encounter she'd had with one particular doctor. Gradually, her feelings began coming out. Her anger was directed at Dr. X. This was a good means of ventilating it and was also justified, since he'd been very rude to her, perhaps because of his own uneasiness at the death. I tried to let her know it was all right to feel angry, to cry and even scream.

Three months later, she was told she had an ulcer. And then she began telling me that things were sinking in, that she was sure she wouldn't make it without her husband, that she felt ashamed she was "falling apart." I assured her that her behavior was normal, kept encouraging her to express her feelings, told her that I was not afraid of them and that I believed she was a strong and good woman.

Today, 6 months after his death, she is beginning to find the strength to start over again. She's becoming active socially once more and, as the grief process works in its normal fashion, is seeing things in proper perspective.

As professionals, we have to be extremely conscious of our own feelings getting in the way. Denial is a normal part of the grieving process, something that's easier to recognize in others than in yourself. And yet we must recognize it in ourselves if we're to continue functioning in helpful ways.

Aftermath of death

Obviously, as this case illustrates, the importance of following up the bereaved family cannot be stressed too much. Grief can take so many destructive paths.

Dr. Elisabeth Kübler-Ross, for instance, states that 70% of the parents of children who died are in the process of separation or divorce within a year after the death. Why? Typically, the father has gone back to work; his other interests take the edge off the pain. Mother remains home, still in a state of shock and perhaps denial. When the father comes home, he finds housework not done, supper not ready, his wife burdened with guilt and grief. Rather than support one another, they fight and blame each other. Often their anger is displaced on the living children.

We can do much to prevent or heal such problems. And as we work with the families, we must not forget — as we so often do — the children, especially the quiet good ones. They need to have their grief and guilt recognized when they lose a loved one. All children occasionally "wish" Mom or Dad or someone close to them were dead; and, if someone dies, they need to be able to distinguish between wish and reality, need to know that the wish did not cause the death. For example, I remember hearing about a little boy who seemed so good and adjusted after his mother died. Every night, though, he put an apple out on his window sill. When questioned about this, he replied, "Mommy loves apples and maybe if I keep putting them out she won't be mad at me anymore and she'll come home."

As with the dying patient, the most helpful approaches in working with the bereaved are the reaffirmation of their lives and your own ability to be comfortable with them. One of the best concepts to share with them is an ancient Russian belief. Incorporated in this belief is the idea that when a person dies, those who are left behind are responsible forever for doing the good he would have done had he lived. This legacy of responsibility is something people can hold onto for as long as they live. It not only gives them "permission," but makes it imperative for them to keep on.

But whatever we do, if we really believe and "live" our vocation, our deep investment of compassion and empathy will be communicated to the bereaved. It can help them find the inner strength in each of us but which, in their despair, they're either blind to or have forgotten.

Thus, even in time of death, we become instruments of healing.

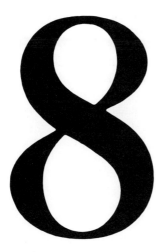

Family support in action

ORA PRATTES

WHEN I WAS A STUDENT, experienced nurses advised me, "Keep your professional distance." The reason was to avoid being hurt, for being hurt weakened you as a nurse.

Over the years, I've questioned this advice. Sure, we do get hurt when we get involved, but I believe the experience leaves us a little stronger. Still, I wondered what effect this "personal" nursing had on the patient and his family. Recently, I had a chance to find out. My experience, I hope, will help you in your dealings with families of the dying.

Last spring, one of my patients, 7-year-old Mike R., died from a malignant tumor in the brain stem after fighting it for 18 months. During his final months and after his death, I had many talks with his mother about Mike, particularly his nursing care. Here, with Mrs. R.'s permission, are excerpts from our tape-recorded conversations:

"Well, Mike seemed fine when he started first grade in September 1970. But early in October he began to trip himself frequently, and on his school papers his printing began running downhill. It hadn't in September. A week later, Mike complained of weakness in his right arm. At the table he began using his left hand. His grin turned lopsided.

"My husband and I knew something was seriously wrong,

*but we decided to wait one more week for him to get better. I
began giving him vitamins each day.''*

Mrs. R.'s initial denial seems clear. Despite Mike's alarming
symptoms, she tried to cure him with vitamins before calling
the doctor. The parents of dying children frequently experience denial and all the other stages of the grieving process as
outlined by Doctor Elisabeth Kübler-Ross: denial, anger, bargaining, depression, acceptance. Some parents bypass some
stages or go through all stages but in a different order. The
nurse should ascertain which stage the parents are in, so that
she can communicate effectively with them. Parents fail to
reach the acceptance stage if they fixate at an earlier stage.
Having failed to accept the inevitability of death, they may be
overwhelmed when the child does die and thus require a great
deal of support as the end draws near.

From denial to bargaining

As we will see, Mrs. R. returned to the denial stage during a
period of false hope. This is common with parents of a terminally ill child who goes into remission.

*"After a week, Mike was no better. Frightened, I called the
doctor, who told me to come in a few days. I argued with him,
told him I couldn't wait, and then I called a friend who got me
an appointment that day with her doctor.''*

Mrs. R. quickly dropped the denial. She became angry
when her doctor refused to see Mike immediately. Her anger
may have been prompted by her guilt over her own delaying,
or it may have been simply a progression to the anger stage of
grieving. At any rate, she was through playing games.

*"That same afternoon, my friend's doctor got me a
neurosurgeon who found Mike had a brain stem tumor. He
explained that such tumors are inoperable and that victims
usually survive for one-and-a-half to two years with treatment.
He said that Mike would need a shunt put in his head to relieve
the pressure the tumor was causing, plus radiotherapy and
chemotherapy with methotrexate.*

*"I told Mike he had a little sore in his brain. And I told him
we were going to make it heal, but that he would have to do just
what the doctor told him. I told the doctor, 'Just tell me what
you want Mike to do, and I'll explain it to him.'''*

Mrs. R. showed great courage even in the beginning of
Mike's treatment. True to her word, she explained to Mike
what was expected of him each step of the way. She reinforced

everything the doctors and nurses told him, often adding, "I know you don't like this, but we have to do it so that the sore in your brain will get well."

An intelligent woman, she understood that Mike's cancer was incurable, yet her constant repetition to Mike that following orders would make his "sore" heal, suggested she yearned to win back his good health through perfect cooperation. This is similar to the bargaining of dying patients who respond to all instructions with a firm, "Just tell me what to do."

"Mike always wanted the same nurse to give his shots. In her absence other nurses had to do it but, with one exception, he didn't trust them the way he did his favorite nurse. He would tell her exactly how to give the shots. He would say, 'Now do this, now do that. Wait, I'm not ready. Okay, now I'm ready.' And she would follow his instructions."

We believe in the value of continuity of nursing care. Even when Mike was being treated later as an outpatient, we still had him return to the pediatric ward for injections because we believe that it is easier for children and that they cooperate more with people they know.

We have found that sick children derive great comfort from rituals, so we follow them closely when possible. Mike needed to direct the entire injection procedure, and we supported his need. While manipulation gives patients a feeling of independence lost during illness, we must establish boundaries of behavior for children so that we do not overindulge them.

"There was one nurse Mike didn't like at all, and I didn't either – one of the men. He never kidded around as all other nurses did. He seemed to want to leave Mike's room as fast as he could. I worried that he might be on duty the day something happened to Mike."

I'm sure this nurse would be amazed to learn that he appeared cold and disinterested to Mrs. R. One day I asked him why he was always in such a hurry to get out of Mike's room. He said, "I just couldn't stay. If I did, I'd cry, and Mike's mother would feel she had to support me. She is so strong and I am not." When I told him I had cried with patients before, he was incredulous. Although he would never agree with me, I believe that nurses ought to realize that sharing their feelings is not only acceptable but is also comforting to the family.

After I heard that Mrs. R. didn't have confidence in this nurse, I assigned his team to the other side. I didn't question his ability; I just provided nurses whom Mrs. R. trusted.

We have found that sick children derive great comfort from rituals, so we follow them closely when possible. Mike needed to direct the entire injection procedure, and we supported his need. While manipulation gives patients a feeling of independence lost during illness, we must establish boundaries of behavior for children so we do not overindulge them.

Giving the family an active role in the care of their hospitalized loved one helps preserve their relationship, a comfort for both. But, though relieved of some nursing chores, the nurse still must supervise the care and provide continuing emotional support for the family and the patient.

During Mike's stay in the hospital, we gave Mrs. R. much responsibility for his care. Besides bathing and feeding him, she gave him the physical therapy exercises and, during his coma, learned to use the suction machine. I asked her if she ever felt we neglected her by allowing her to assume so much responsibility for Mike's care.

"No, the nurses came in several times a day. I would be exercising one arm, and they'd grab the other, and we'd visit and work together. Also, most of his doctors and nurses came in every day to buy some gum from Mike's gumball machine; they would joke with us about how Mike made them buy gum from him."

Giving the family an active role in the care of their hospitalized loved one helps preserve their relationship, a comfort to both. Though relieved of some nursing chores, the nurse still must supervise the care and provide continuing emotional support for the family and the patient.

"After a few weeks, Mike's symptoms disappeared, and he went back to school while continuing treatment as an outpatient. Mike did well in school, but shortly after beginning second grade, he began having bad headaches. I would put baby aspirin in his pocket and tell him to take them if his headache got real bad. Some days he wouldn't have to take them, and he would be so proud."

Avoiding overindulgence is especially important to get across to the family, who should be led to realize their loved one, particularly if he is a child, is comforted by continuing his normal activities for as long as his condition permits. Once Mrs. R. learned that the headaches were unavoidable because the increasing pressure could no longer be relieved, she and Mike courageously took steps to relieve his pain with aspirin so that he could stay in school.

"By January of 1972, Mike was frequently experiencing bad days. He would come home and lie down or become cross with the other children, not his usual behavior.

"One day he developed a 103° fever and had to be admitted to the hospital. The old shunt had become infected and the surgeon had to put in a new one on the other side.

"Two months later, Mike was visiting a friend's home, when he lapsed into a coma. I rushed him to the hospital emergency room and told the nurse to call a neurosurgeon. I explained that Mike had a brain tumor and was in a coma. She took Mike into another room and gave me some forms to fill out. I told

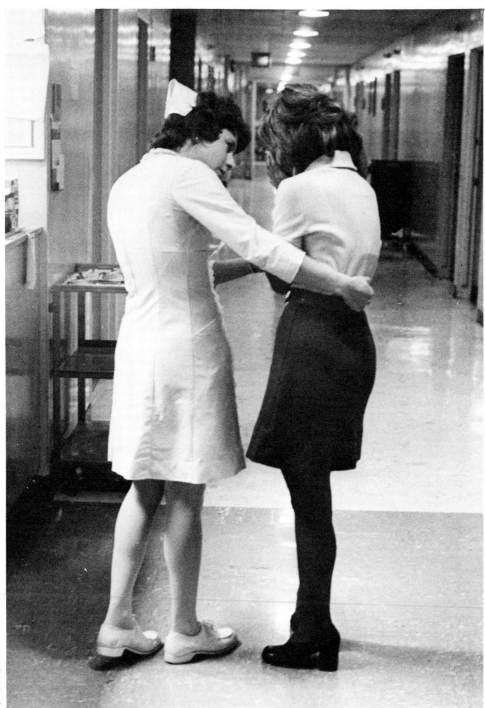

another nurse, 'Just tell me where to sign; I have to be with Mike.' When the nurse insisted I complete the forms, I just put them down and rushed back to Mike. I thought he was dying. The nurse threatened to call a security guard to have me evicted, but I still refused to leave.

"I was almost hysterical. The nurse was probably afraid I'd break down and get in the way. But I knew I wouldn't, and I just couldn't understand how they could expect me to sit in another room, filling out forms, while Mike was dying.

"The nurse left to get the doctor, I think, and Mike started a funny chewing motion. There wasn't any food or gum in his mouth, so I called, 'Come quick. He's having a seizure.'

"The nurse just looked at me, not at him, and said, 'How would you know? Has he had one before?' Then she did look at him, and put a padded tongue depressor in his mouth.

"The doctor was new, and he didn't know Mike's history. I had had that experience before, and I kept a notebook with me at all times with Mike's whole medical history in it. He took the history and admitted Mike. After that day, I also kept a padded tongue depressor in my purse."

The nurse's dealings with Mrs. R. were not only insensitive, they also demeaned her intelligence, with the demand, "How would you know?" This attitude is ridiculous when you consider that the next moment the doctor would be admitting Mike based on Mrs. R.'s recollection of his medical history. I asked Mrs. R. if she had had other instances of frustration with hospital personnel not familiar with Mike's history.

"Most everyone was nice, but at times I would get frustrated. Once, after the operation to replace Mike's shunt, the doctor told me Mike could have a regular diet for dinner. But when I went to get Mike's tray, the nurse said she couldn't give him one because the doctor hadn't written it down. I just felt helpless, knowing that the doctor meant for Mike to have food. So I sent my older son to the cafeteria to buy a sandwich.

"Another time, I went home to rest. I called the ward later to ask how Mike was doing, and the clerk told me she was forbidden to give information over the phone. After that I asked to speak to the nurses; they told me everything."

In both these instances I think the people let the rules override good judgment. Not writing an order was the doctor's fault, but many nurses would have had the courage to give Mike a dinner tray, knowing Mrs. R. to be competent and intelligent. Doubting her word, for want of a signed order, undermined her feeling of being able to care for her son. As she said, "I just felt helpless."

Her telephone request for information was another example. After hearing about it, I wrote on Mike's Kardex, "Mrs. R. is to be told everything she wants to know at any time." We didn't have any more trouble. Mrs. R. recounted another incident that caused her to become even more angry.

"Then, in April while Mike was in the coma, he began running a high fever. A doctor told me Mike had pneumonia, and he would treat it with antibiotics. I had to stay home that night and the next morning to look after the other children. The next afternoon, when I came back, Mike's temperature was still very high. I asked about the antibiotics and the nurse looked at me, surprised, and said, 'Mike is not on antibiotics.' I got upset then, and called the doctor. He explained that the tumor was growing more rapidly now and the doctors had decided that giving Mike antibiotics couldn't really help him and might prolong his suffering.

"I blew up. I called him unethical and a lot of other things. All I could think of was that Mike had a simple disease that they could easily cure, and they were letting him die.

"After I got home, I felt ashamed. I understood what the doctor was trying to say, and I called him to apologize."

Mike had been in a coma for 4 weeks at this time, and the strain on the family was becoming unbearable. The nursing staff encouraged Mrs. R. to go home as much as possible both to give herself badly needed rest and to take care of her family, which she had been neglecting for over a year.

Part of her anger probably reflects her guilt at being away. She may have believed that had she stayed at the hospital, the antibiotics would have been given. But her anger also reflects a recurrence of the denial we saw earlier. Her thoughts focused on the pneumonia: "a simple disease, easily cured." Her will to deny the existence of a fatal tumor was growing stronger as Mike's condition deteriorated. I asked Mrs. R. if the nurses were able to help her while Mike was in the coma.

"Yes, the nurses came in the room a lot; when they could, they would stay and visit. I got to know them well, to know about their families and their problems. I felt I could count on them because I knew they cared about Mike. One nurse talked to me so much, she was like a friend. One day when Mike was very bad, she told me, 'When things happen, I want to be here with Mike, but I also don't.' One of the attendants wanted to

Mike had been in a coma for 4 weeks, and the strain on the family was becoming unbearable. The nursing staff encouraged Mrs. R. to go home as much as possible both to give herself badly needed rest and to take care of her family, which she had been neglecting for over a year.

help, I think, but he made me nervous by coming in and out and asking me if I needed anything. He finally asked me if I wanted some coffee. I didn't, but I found myself saying 'yes' to make him feel better."

During Mike's hospitalization a number of children had died from kidney trouble, children Mrs. R. had gotten to know. One afternoon she called me about the possibility of her donating Mike's kidneys for transplants to another child. She had discussed this with her family, and it was agreeable to them. She had made this decision on her own. All the necessary papers had been signed, and members of the transplant team were notified when death was imminent. When Cheyne-Stokes respiration began, Mike was moved to the ICU, where he was to be monitored and ventilated until his heart stopped and he was removed to the operating suite. Here is how Mrs. R. described that last day.

"I had just gone home to take a bath, and the nurse called and asked us to come in. I told my husband. 'We have to hurry; Mike is dying.' I felt sure of it.

"When we got to the ward, a lot of nurses and doctors were in Mike's room. My husband and I went in, and the transplant team crowded around. We knew we were in the way, so we went out in the hall.

"The orderly kept looking at me and then looking away. He still wanted to say something to comfort me, but he couldn't. I was worrying about how I was going to react at the last moment. You know the last moment is coming, but you don't want it to ever get there.

"I knew all the nurses in Mike's room, and I felt some comfort in that. I stood in the hall, looking in, and I was terribly worried that I would lose control of myself. The nurse I knew so well came over and stood by me quietly. I said to her, 'I'm going to be all right.'

"'Don't worry. We understand,' she said. I looked at her and I realized that she was crying a little.

"Seeing that she could cry comforted me. I remember thinking, 'She isn't even Mike's mother. If she can cry, why can't I?' I cried then for the first time. I couldn't have if she hadn't been ready to shed some tears, too. Mike died that day. Eighteen months after the diagnosis. He had been in a coma for 8 weeks and 2 hours.

"Most of the nurses who cared for Mike were able to attend the funeral, which comforted me. I felt proud too – that they

had come, with all the work they had to do. Mike had been such a joy to us; I knew, when I saw the nurses there, that he had become an important part of them too."

I don't think we are ever ready for a patient, particularly a child, to die, and the funeral offers a therapeutic way for the nurses to resolve their grief. It's appropriate to cry at funerals, and many of the nurses did.

Resolution through sharing

We had to go to the funeral in our uniforms, which made me feel uncomfortable at first. But it demonstrated my belief that there's nothing unprofessional about becoming involved.

"About 2 weeks after the funeral, the nurse who had been closest to me phoned and we talked for about 2 hours. I visited the hospital later and had lunch with all the nurses. They told me that a little girl with a brain tumor, a girl I'd seen when visiting Mike, was back in the hospital. I wanted to comfort her, so I brought a teddy bear for her. She could not speak; she kissed me, and I cried. I could see Mike all over again. I wanted to say so much to the mother, and I'd prepared myself at home to say it. But when I saw her, I had such a lump in my throat that I couldn't talk. I just left. I went downtown on the bus, and bought a religious medal and I took the bus back and gave it to her."

Mrs. R. could now understand why the male nurse and the orderly had been unable to talk with her during Mike's final days. The fact that she could still feel such an overwhelming grief and sympathy for another child's mother shows that her own loss had not left her bitter.

Mrs. R. is an unusually strong, religious person. Her own resourcefulness, her ability to articulate and to understand the nature of Mike's disease — all were great assets. Because of these strengths, she was able to make necessary decisions and to prepare herself and her family for Mike's death. But what about the relatives who cannot articulate so well and do not understand the disease or the health care system as Mrs. R. did? How will they cope with emergencies, especially when confronted by hospital personnel unfamiliar with their loved one's medical history? In such cases, continuity of care from the same nurses is even more important than it was for Mrs. R. Only through such continuity can they provide maximum support for these families and then only if they shed some of their so-called professionalism and become truly involved.

SKILLCHECK 2

Like the situations in Skillcheck 1, these questions have a variety of possible answers. Write down all that you can imagine to test — and to further develop — your problem-solving skills.

1. Mr. Schwartz, a gentleman in his 60s, seems finally to have come to accept his death. But his wife and children haven't. They constantly tell him that he can't die now — they need him too much. This is making death more difficult for Mr. Schwartz.

How would you approach the family?

2. While talking to you, Mrs. Young, whose husband has just died suddenly in the emergency room from a car accident, begins sobbing uncontrollably. "I feel so guilty," she says. "The last time I saw him this morning, we had a tremendous argument. I never had a chance to tell him I was sorry for getting angry."

How might you help her?

3. Bobbie, a lovely 7-year-old girl with cystic fibrosis, seems to sense that she is dying. But her parents refuse to

discuss the subject with her or to face the possibility themselves.

How could you approach them?

4. The family of Mrs. Washington, a cancer patient, has been unusually vigilant and loving. While they are in the coffee shop for a short lunch, though, Mrs. Washington dies with difficulty and asking for her youngest son. When the family returns and learns of her death, they tearfully ask whether she suffered and asked for any of them.

What are some appropriate responses?

Answer the following with brief essays.

5. You walk into the room of a 15-year-old unwed mother (Catholic) who has been severely burned and witnessed the fiery death of her boyfriend. When she sees you, she begins to cry, saying, "Jesus had to die on the cross because people like me have babies without being married."

What is your emotional response? What do you say to her?

6. Write a letter of condolence to a newly bereaved person.

Dealing with yourself and the staff

Living with dying

JEANNE BRIMIGION

SHOULD WE EVER CONFRONT a dying patient with the irreversibility of his illness "for his own good"? Should we lie to him if a relative wants us to? Should we always follow a doctor's orders to "do nothing" for a patient, and thereby become an instrument of death by delegation?

These are nearly unanswerable questions. Yet we nurses are forced to ponder them — and, at some time or other during the course of our jobs, forced to answer them through our actions . . . or inaction. Assuming such a profound responsibility can be very stressful for a nursing staff. I know because my nursing post confronts me often with death. But with supportive teamwork and understanding, a staff can cope and give the tender care their patients need.

At our nursing home, the patients average 80 years of age. Most have significant pathology involving several organ systems. Many — a great many — die on the premises.

Needless to say, our nurses become emotionally attached to our patients and their families. And much affected by the decisions they must make regarding them. Consider this patient, for example:

A 74-year-old man was admitted with metastatic carcinoma of the prostate. He had urethral stricture with acute urinary tract infection, and a permanent indwelling Foley catheter. There were two open decubitus ulcers on his ischial spine and coccyx.

His wife, terminally ill with metastatic carcinoma of the ovaries, was admitted to an adjoining room. She lived for 7 months until death claimed her at age 75.

After his wife's death, the husband's depression and fear increased. Apparently always a demanding and unbending person, he grew more preoccupied with routine and rules. Obsessively so. Medications had to be on time, never a minute late. His enemas and baths had to be regimented as to time and day. He quarreled over any deviation from daily routine.

Many times, the staff discussed whether the patient should conform to our rules or we to his. Then we began to realize that his ritualistic regulation of life was irrevocably tied to his desperate fear of death. As long as he controlled his own life, he evidently felt he was warding off death.

So, we adapted to his demands as much as possible in all areas. It took new insight on the part of the staff to realize that the regimen of the institution is not always in the patient's best interest. During the ensuing months, especially on the anniversary of the wife's death, the patient became morbid and withdrawn. Our staff spent time discussing his feelings and tried to help him sort out his conflicting emotions.

When he became terminally ill, four of his five children were on an extended trip. One daughter arrived and spent a great deal of time at his bedside.

Staff members who knew him well were assigned to stay with him; other personnel spent time with his daughter to support her during the death vigil. On the last day, he was never left alone. When he began to verbalize the knowledge of impending death, the staff agreed, saying, "Yes, you are dying but you are not alone." These gestures seemed to help alleviate his fear somewhat.

After his death, we assisted with funeral arrangements. Because the family was away, the patient was buried very simply and some of the staff members attended the services.

Impediments to involvement   During this particular case, we gradually grew more aware of what nurses' roles with the dying could be. We began to question our involvement in the death process, its effect on families, and its impact on other patients. Our first realization was this: We are very involved in the death process. Caring for the dying patient is a great challenge that is given to very few of us. Death is the final act of life, and a person dies very much alone and frightened. We are given the special opportunity to aid and comfort the dying and also provide comfort and understanding to family members.

We daily live with death and should willingly face the fact, for it adds a new dimension to our nursing goals.

A major hurdle was the staff's attitude. Our nurses had been trained not to speak about death. When a patient was transferred to the hospital and died there, they would tell inquiring patients, "He's coming along," or, "He's doing better." Later, when the death notice appeared in the local paper, the residents resented the staff's lies.

When patients died in our facility, requests by residents to view the body had always been denied. The nurses avoided speaking about death, causing one patient to comment, "That's how they are going to treat me. I will be forgotten so soon!"

Many of our nonprofessional staff come from varied cultures, and death is shrouded in superstition and symbolism. Much understanding and education are necessary to alter attitudes and fears established over a lifetime.

And it was not easy to decide which patients wanted to talk about critical illness and death, and which didn't. We had to find ways for those who wanted to communicate to do so without involving those who wanted to avoid the issue.

The third problem — besides the staff's and patients' attitudes — related to the families. Some relatives are overly troubled by impending death, to the point of becoming irrational and hysterical, thereby upsetting the patient further. Others say that, for them, the relative has been more dead than alive for a long time and that actual physical death would be an anticlimax. Other relatives simply want the secret of terminal illness kept; that cuts us off completely from being able to honestly answer questions such as, "Do I have cancer?" . . . "What is wrong with me?" . . . "Am I going to die?" We, therefore, must spend time with families helping them come to terms with irreversible illness.

A fourth problem was with physicians. All patients have private physicians, who hold varied attitudes toward the terminal aged patient. Some are very dedicated to continuation of life for as long as possible. Others feel that once a terminal

Death is the final act of life, and a person dies very much alone and frightened. We are given the special opportunity to aid and comfort the dying and also provide comfort and understanding to family members. We daily live with death and should face the fact, for it adds a new dimension to our nursing goals.

condition is present, a patient should be made comfortable and no "extreme measures" should be taken to continue the life process. We in the institution are having a great deal of difficulty trying to interpret the meaning of "extreme measures." Because we are concerned with helping our patients perform to their maximum potential, however limited it may be, we are geared to cultivating the seed of "life" and we minimize disabilities as much as possible.

There are some special problems facing the nursing staff who have direct contact with the terminally ill patient and around-the-clock responsibility for his care. For example: consider a patient who is dysphagic or semicomatose and cannot swallow. The physician may not feel he can write orders that provide alternative feeding methods such as clysis, I.V.s, or nasogastric tube, or a definite nursing program. He may say, "Do nothing" or "Make him comfortable." This "Do nothing" attitude upsets many of us because we feel that by withholding food, exercise, and stimuli we speed up the dying process. Therefore, we may contribute to death by neglecting the things necessary to continue life, and we object to becoming the instrument of death by delegation.

Sharing the grief   Despite these various problems, our administration and staff slowly began to explore solutions. I would like to share the techniques we have developed over the past several years:

• We hold intensive inservice training for all staff members on death and dying, covering these areas:

Who speaks for the patient: The family? The doctor? The institution? The patient himself?

What are some of our built-in fears toward illness and death? Do we communicate those feelings to others? What effect does our attitude have on patients, on staff members, and on members of families?

How can we communicate to others our deep feelings for life, so they better understand our position?

• We encourage the staff to listen to patients discuss real feelings and fears, and to always seem willing to listen.

• At group therapy sessions each Saturday morning, patients meet with our staff psychologist and Director of Nursing Services. They're encouraged to talk about their concerns and share their fears. Many times, they find support and help in bearing their own illnesses. The group functions as a therapeutic tool, as patients learn to support and counsel each other. Some areas discussed by the group: death, illness, feelings of abandonment, isolation. Sometimes, patients who've been active participants become ill, then return to the group more disabled. The group may not be prepared to accept the new handicap and feels uncomfortable in the presence of feeding tubes, increased aphasia, or paralysis. Discussions center around what is best for the particular patient and the group. Participants seek solutions concerning disagreement on whether the needs of the minority (the disabled patient) or the majority (the group) should be served.

• All staff members are encouraged to deal with a patient's relatives frankly and honestly. Changes in a patient's condition are discussed with the family, and new treatments and procedures are explained simply. We all try to alleviate the suspicion and fear that certain treatments seem to provoke in family members.

We also alert them to possible side effects and expected benefits. If a sudden downhill change occurs and the family is not present, we usually call them to give the opportunity to visit if they wish.

• When a patient becomes critically ill, and death seems imminent, a rotation staff is provided to be with the patient almost constantly. Extra time is spent caring for his physical and medical needs, as well as giving emotional support and personal contact. He is encouraged to talk or be silent if he wishes, but is reassured that he is not alone and his mood will be respected.

• The patient's clergyman is called and asked to spend as much time as he can with the patient during the final hours.

• When the relatives do not live in the vicinity, we can assist in making funeral arrangements locally or helping expedite whatever formalities are needed for taking a body across county and state lines.

• When the viewing and funeral services are held locally, our staff members closest to the deceased are given time off and encouraged to attend. If services are elsewhere, cards signed by the staff are routinely sent to the family.

• Other patients who were attached to the dying patient are encouraged to visit him. When death occurs and the deceased has been properly cared for, they are allowed to come in and see him before he is taken to the funeral home.

• Our nursing home holds three worship services each week

When a patient becomes critically ill, and death seems imminent, a rotation staff is provided to be with the patient almost constantly. Extra time is spent caring for his physical and medical needs, as well as giving emotional support and personal contact. He is encouraged to talk or be silent if he wishes, but is reassured that he is not alone and his mood will be respected.

for three major faiths. Most patients who can, do attend services, regardless of religious background. Each clergyman takes the ecumenical aspect of our group into consideration. We have found this an appropriate place for patients to discuss some of their fears and concerns about living and dying. When a patient dies, the pastor mentions it. Residents and staff are encouraged to share their remembrances of the patient with the group. There is a common sharing of grief, which brings everyone closer together. Each patient knows that if he dies, he will in turn be remembered by friends at the home.

• We publish a monthly newsletter covering all areas of our life, new admissions, new staff, special projects and programs. Included is a simple recognition of all deaths, with expressions of sympathy to family and friends.

• The Medical Director and I meet with all staff responsible for the deceased patient's care. This includes housekeepers, dietitians, special service personnel, recreational personnel, and nurses. We thank them for a job well done and discuss areas of improvement for similar patients we now have or expect to have.

From our work have emerged plans for several other actions:

• Joint meetings between staff and attending physicians, to encourage physicians to spend more time with patients discussing emotional and psychological conditions as well as physical conditions.

• Special sensitivity-training programs for volunteers. We plan to train people of all ages interested in visiting work and in encouraging realistic and objective dealings on patients' terms with things most on their minds.

• A Bereavement Clinic for surviving family members to provide an understanding and supportive atmosphere during the trying months following death.

Indeed, dealing with dying patients has taught us much about living. We hope to keep learning, for there is much to learn about both life and death.

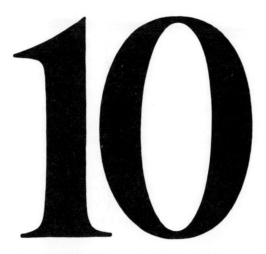

Comforting each other

SHEILA LELLY BLAKE

A PRACTICAL NURSE ONCE SAID to me, "All your theory on death and dying is fine. But you also have to be *people* with your patients."

I agree. But I'd take her statement one step further — you also have to be "people" with yourself and other staff members. Because, like our patients and their families, we nurses respond to death and dying with grief — and we too need help to work through it.

I'm thinking here about our staff's reaction to so many patients whom we've watched struggling to survive. Carl Baden, for instance — a handsome 30-year-old leukemic still on our unit, but for how long?

Carl was in successful remission two years ago. But he stopped taking his medication and skipped his clinic check-ups. By the time he finally returned to the clinic, he had serious central nervous system symptoms — paresthesia of the face, arms, and legs and severe personality changes. Chemotherapy and radiation cleared up his symptoms for a couple of months. But then they returned, and they've grown continually worse since.

When Carl first came to our unit as an inpatient, he was still a personable and optimistic young man with lots of attentive girlfriends. But in the past six months, he's changed totally. Now he spends his days alone, watching television, talking little, and sunk in utter depression. His personality and appearance have changed so drastically that no one visits.

Witnessing Carl's physical and emotional deterioration has been agonizing for us. We've felt angry and depressed over our inability to halt the progressive neurological involvement, frustrated by our inability to find friends to visit him, and still hopeful that, despite his prognosis, somehow he'll get better.

These feelings — anger, depression, hope — are just as surely stages of grief as Carl's denial and despair. I'm convinced that they're natural, maybe even necessary feelings for sensitive nurses. After all, how can we expect to share deep emotions with a patient or family one minute if we reject our own tears of joy or sadness the next?

I've always considered unrealistic the idea that nurses should feel, care, be sensitive to patients' needs and at the same time ignore their own needs or maintain constant composure. If you care about your patients, you'll never achieve that kind of emotional balance. Each time you think you've "got it together," something or someone will touch you deeply enough to challenge your emotional equilibrium. And I think that's okay, because with each challenge you grow professionally and personally. But how can you cope with intense emotional involvement day after day, patient after patient?

During the 18 months that we've worked together as an oncology unit, I think we've asked ourselves that question hundreds of times. It's taken us nearly a year to accept the fact that no pat answers exist — that each of us has to cope in our own way and do our own soul-searching. But in those months we've also discovered that, if we dare to be forthright about our feelings of fear, inadequacy, and doubt, we can help each other through the emotional valleys.

No one is an island

On any unit where death threatens, no one can afford to remain aloof from other staff members. You have to share heavy emotional demands if you want to avoid emotional debilitation.

I'm not suggesting that you can completely shoulder someone else's burdens — or that they can completely shoulder yours. Far from it. But, if you're willing to talk openly, to admit your fears and doubts, and to listen sympathetically, you can at least lighten each other's burdens.

Don't expect to accomplish this immediately, though. Learning to listen and talk openly takes time, humility, and trust. When our unit first opened, we established group sessions led by a psychologically trained person so the staff nurses would have a place to ventilate their feelings. But the early sessions fell short of our expectations. Instead of being group therapy, they became little more than group accusations. Because they didn't know each other well and feared that the others would interpret their fears as failures, the staff blamed difficulties with patients on other groups — "If only the doctors wouldn't do this," they would say. Or, "If only housekeeping would do that." They were very careful to steer the conversation away from themselves by blaming "safe" people who weren't present.

These scapegoat sessions persisted for almost two months. Then, someone finally blurted out, "Well, I've been working with Mr. Adams and *I'm* beginning to feel really inadequate." Only then did the staff begin opening up — they knew that their feelings of inadequacy weren't abnormal. Once the sessions got underway, I bowed out of them. I feel that a staff should have one place where they can say anything without fear of censure from their supervisors. So, I reserve my interactions for our weekly staff conferences.

Now, all of the nurses rely heavily on the sessions as a place to ventilate their feelings and explore new approaches to their difficulties. They meet once a week for one hour on each shift. During that hour, research nurses, student nurses, and available supervisory staff take over patient care.

The group sessions have truly become the staff's meetings. For example, even though I nominate a new leader whenever the existing one rotates off our unit, they hold the final vote of approval. And even though the leader (psychiatrist, psychologist, psychiatric nurse, or chaplain) usually opens each session by asking what problems everyone has encountered since the last meeting, the group itself generally steers the discussion. Occasionally the leader may intervene to interpret feelings or suggest new perspectives. But most of the support comes from the group itself in their sympathy and friendship.

As helpful as group sessions are, though, they can't meet day-to-day problems. They just can't meet often enough.

When you feel frustrated because a patient doesn't get a

If you're willing to talk openly, to admit your fears and doubts, and to listen sympathetically, you can at least lighten each other's burdens. Don't expect to accomplish this immediately, though. Learning to listen and talk openly takes time, humility, and trust.

response to chemotherapy, or because he wants to go home but no one's there to take care of him; when you feel angry because a patient tells you he wants no more treatment, yet tells the physician, "Do everything you can"; when you feel angry, guilty, and frustrated because you think you're no longer prolonging life but instead prolonging death; when you feel sad, hurt, and even relieved at losing or having lost a patient; when you feel that wry combination of relief and rejection because you've made a special effort to reach a patient yet he's chosen someone else to confide in — these are the times when you need immediate support. If you don't deal with your feelings on the spot, they can become debilitating, affecting your relationships with other patients, other staff members, and sometimes even your family.

To cope with feelings like these, you have to learn to share them on a one-to-one level. This takes a keen sensitivity to each other and an awareness of how each of you expresses your emotions. Remember that not everyone expresses her feelings in the same way. Some express fear and doubt as irritability, for instance; others, as depression; still others, as distraction; and so on.

I believe that staff meetings can be particularly helpful in teaching a staff to detect the personal signs of depression, discomfort, anger, frustration, or fatigue in each other. But even if a unit doesn't have staff meetings, you can learn to identify those signs if you make a conscious effort to keep an eye on each other. Then, if someone is really "down," someone who is "up" can reach out to her.

Reaching out may entail nothing more than listening or helping to identify a problem. Recently, for instance, I was standing with a young graduate at the elevators. When I asked her how things were going, she said, "Oh, I'm so mad at these elevators. They're so slow they're going to do me in someday."

I agreed that sometimes they do test your patience. But I added that usually they're upsetting when something else is bothering you.

"Well," she said, "as a matter of fact, I've come to the end of my rope with one of my patients. No matter what I do, it seems to be wrong for him. I feel I should know how to make him happy. But I don't."

I asked her if she'd asked him what he was so angry about. She said no. Then she thought for a few seconds and said,

"You know, I just assumed that he didn't like me. I hadn't thought about the fact that he might be upset about something else. Maybe I should try to talk with him."

In that case, just talking about the situation gave the nurse the perspective she needed to deal with her feelings. That isn't always enough, though. Sometimes you have to give the other person time, too. For example, one very busy day a few months ago our head nurse assigned herself to several patients. Suddenly one of her ambulatory patients began hemorrhaging from her lungs; an artery had exploded. The staff was helpless, so the head nurse assumed command. At her direction, the staff attempted suctioning, but the faster they suctioned, the more blood poured from the patient's mouth. The patient died very traumatically. Even though the staff pitched in to help the head nurse clean the patient and the room, which were covered with blood, the head nurse bore the brunt of the

To cope with feelings, you have to learn to share them on a one-to-one basis. This takes a keen sensitivity to each other and an awareness of how each of you expresses your emotions. Remember that not everyone expresses her feelings in the same way.

emotional trauma. When a research nurse heard about the situation, she came to relieve the head nurse for half an hour. She felt that the head nurse needed to get off the area for a while.

In that case, talking just wouldn't have been enough to help the nurse cope with her feelings. The emotional trauma was so overwhelming that she really needed to escape, if only briefly.

Sometimes, in fact, an entire staff may need to escape. Recently we had a situation like that. One of our patients, Mr. Sanderson, had a large tumor over and surrounding his trachea. The tumor's position made establishment of an airway, either with a tracheostomy or an endotracheal tube, medically impossible. Mr. Sanderson was slowly suffocating, and we were helpless to alleviate his suffering. Watching this man's agony was extremely painful for us. We knew he wanted someone with him constantly, but expecting one person to stay in attendance was an almost inhuman request. Spontaneously, the staff devised its own solution: They maintained a vigil at his bedside but relieved each other at frequent intervals. Throughout Mr. Sanderson's last 24 hours, they continued their rotation, passing it along from shift to shift. Maybe he didn't die painlessly, but at least he didn't die alone.

I don't think the staff ever could've arrived at this type of solution if they hadn't been so well attuned to each other's feelings and so willing to admit their emotional limitations. They've learned one of the most vital messages of nursing: No one can function alone around dying patients.

Identifying feelings

Group meetings and personal rapport can help you cope with fears and doubts by giving you a chance to "blow up," to get everything off your chest. But we've found that they help in another way, too: They can give you clues to the feelings you're likely to experience.

The following are the three that we've found to be most common on our unit. Knowing our experiences may not prevent you from having similar ones. But it may help you to mentally prepare yourself for them — and when they come, to know that, as difficult and persistent as your feelings seem, they are a normal and healthy part of good nursing.

Guilt. Of all the problems that we encounter, we seem to have the most difficulty dealing with guilt. Guilt can come from a thousand different sources — our anger with a patient or family, refusal to meet all of their demands, inability to meet all of their needs, a patient's anger at us, and so on. Sometimes our action — or inaction — was a conscious choice that we felt was in the patient's or family's best interest; sometimes it came from a simple error in judgment. What makes guilt so difficult in all cases, though, is that so often you can't take any specific action to absolve it. You can try to "make up" for the action. But only time, and the understanding and acceptance that time brings, seems to truly resolve the feeling.

Not long ago, we had a patient whose family had maintained a constant vigil at his bedside. One afternoon a nursing assistant had to clean the patient, who was incontinent. Before going into his room, she asked several nurses whether she should ask the family to step outside or allow them to stay. Everyone told her to ask them to step outside for just five minutes. She did, and while they were absent, the patient died.

Understandably, the family was upset that they couldn't be with the patient in his final minutes. But the event was nearly as traumatic for the nursing assistant, who felt guilty for having "deprived" the patient and the family of a meaningful moment.

In tears she said, "Why did I listen to everyone else? Why didn't I follow my own gut feeling to let them stay? I feel so sorry for the family."

For weeks she mourned over the situation. We tried to reassure her that she had no way of knowing that the patient would die at that moment. But nothing seemed to help her.

In time, however, she gained a new perspective on the situation. During a conversation with another nurse, she said, "Well, maybe the patient didn't want the family there when he died. I've heard of patients waiting until someone was there to die. Maybe he was waiting until his family was absent."

Even though she still hasn't fully accepted this idea, it has helped her begin to resolve her guilt feelings. Some people might view her explanation as a rationalization, a defense mechanism. Perhaps that's true. But even if it is, that's okay. Sometimes we must use defense mechanisms to protect our emotional equilibrium and to get us through the initial trauma. Later, we can reflect and grow through a more objective analysis.

Analysis of feelings is important. But it takes a long time. The most important thing initially is that we let ourselves feel and that, when we make a mistake, we say to ourselves, "Yes,

Of all the problems that we encounter, we seem to have the most difficulty dealing with guilt. Guilt can come from a thousand different sources. What makes it so difficult in all cases, though, is that so often you can't take any specific action to absolve it. Only time seems to truly resolve the feeling.

To keep yourself going, set short, achievable goals for patients. These might include getting a patient's diet changed to something he really likes, fixing him a cup of coffee before the breakfast cart arrives, relaxing hospital rules to allow him extra sleep. No matter how small the accomplishment, it can make the day good and meaningful for the patient as well as for you.

I misjudged. But I'm only human. And next time, I'll know better what to do."

Inadequacy and helplessness. I wonder if any nurse exists who hasn't felt inadequate and helpless during conversations with dying patients or their families, particularly when they ask questions she can't answer or when she can't give them the hope they're so desperately seeking. Each of us wants to say just the right thing but we don't always succeed.

In our close work with so many patients, though, we've found that it isn't what we say or how we express it that seems to affect the patient, but whether or not we care.

I first learned that lesson from Mr. Colson, a 35-year-old father of four who was awaiting a tissue diagnosis before treatment could begin. Several days elapsed while he underwent a complete metastatic workup. During those days he became more edgy, worrying that his tumor was growing, worrying about who would take care of his wife, his children, and his mother if anything happened to him. He felt as though his life were closing in on him.

One day he told me, "I know I have cancer. But while I'm waiting for the doctors to find out what kind, this tumor just seems to be getting larger and larger."

Since he knew why the tests and waiting were necessary, I didn't need to explain that situation to him. What could I say? Out of my feeling of helplessness, I put my hand on his arm and said, "I feel what you're saying, but I just can't find the words to tell you how well I understand."

At that, he began crying and expressing all his fears and frustrations. I sat and listened. When he finished, I began identifying some specific areas where we could help him. Just letting him know my feelings, I realized, had helped him to open up and eventually come to grips with *his* feelings.

Patients aren't always as fragile as we think. Even if our responses sound harsh or ineffectual to us, the patients will be able to detect our feelings if we really care about them.

Sometimes, though, you may feel helpless because you can't help a patient medically. As with Mr. Sanderson, the patient with the tumor over his trachea, the only relief may be periodic escape from an overwhelming situation. In addition to relief from the floor during the day, we've found that we cope best if we can get three or four days off at fairly frequent intervals. We've found, too, that we can retain our equilibrium better if we have interests outside the hospital. Many of us enjoy hiking, working in the yard, sports, reading, window shopping, and other pastimes. Whatever the form, a diversion can take your mind off your work and revitalize your spirits.

But what about your hours on the job, when you have to confront seemingly hopeless situations day after day? To keep going, set short, achievable goals for patients. These might include getting a patient's diet changed to something he really likes, fixing him a cup of coffee before the breakfast cart arrives, relaxing hospital rules to allow him extra sleep, or arranging for him to see those children that mean so much to him yet are too young to visit the unit officially. No matter how small the accomplishment, it can make the day good and meaningful for the patient as well as for you.

Insensitivity. Every nurse who works regularly with dying patients has to be careful that she doesn't become impatient with the "minor" complaints or problems of her friends and family. When a healthy person complains of feeling trapped in his job, not having enough money for that house he wants, or other disappointments, it's easy to think, "My patients and I are dealing with life and death issues. How can you be so upset over your little problem?" You must make a special effort to maintain your perspective and realize that these problems are very real for those people.

Look for rewards

As we've discovered in the past 18 months, working with dying patients is not an easy job. You must expect moments of sadness and grief, and feelings of helplessness. But working with the dying also can be rewarding, both personally and professionally. The dignity and courage of these patients can give you a new appreciation for life. You'll learn to look for the moments of joy and happiness that you can share with your patients and your co-workers.

Preparing a patient to go home for even a short stay with his loving family . . . celebrating the surprise birthday party that the staff and patients arranged for a young leukemic patient . . . watching a patient who usually won't eat light up with delight at the soda crackers or orange you brought from home . . . having a patient share his memories with you . . . receiving a smile or a pat on the shoulder from a patient, family, or co-worker. These are the rewards that can come from working with dying patients. Strangely enough, they always seem to come when you need them most.

SKILLCHECK 3

Write as many answers as possible to these five questions.

1. Dr. Greenberg is a kind man and an excellent physician but totally incapable of dealing with death. Whenever one of his patients is dying, he becomes brusque with that patient, other patients, and the nursing staff. You like the doctor and don't want to hurt his feelings, but you feel something must be done because he is upsetting the patients and staff.
What are some possible approaches?

2. Mrs. Marks, a 78-year-old former businesswoman, is dying of cancer. You think that she suspects she's dying and that she's emotionally strong enough to know the truth. But the doctor refuses to tell her. Now you find yourself avoiding her because you're afraid she'll ask you about her condition.
How could you improve this situation?

3. You've grown very fond of Mrs. Hansen, a terminally ill patient on your floor. And she obviously is very fond of you, since she often asks for you to care for her. You find caring for her difficult, however, because she reminds you of your mother, who died similarly two years ago.
How could you handle your feelings and the situation?

4. In the past two weeks, four patients on your unit have died. Staff morale has hit an all-time low. What could you do to boost the staff's and your own morale?

5. As a visiting chaplain over the past 6 years, Rev. Sanders has been a tremendous comfort to terminal patients and often to you. Now, though, he himself is a terminal patient on your floor. Despite his obvious pain, he is always cheerful when you enter his room and tells you openly that he fully accepts his impending death. You, however, can't accept the death of this saintly man.
How could you deal with your feelings?

For the following exercises, write essay answers.

6. In one or more paragraphs, complete the following: *When I think of death, I . . . .*

7. Find a quiet place where you can be alone for 15 or 20 minutes. Close your eyes and, for two minutes, concentrate on your own death. Then, write down your feelings.

8. Write your own death notice, eulogy, or funeral sermon.

Some
personal
views

Surviving: Four patients talk

WHAT DOES A PATIENT facing a life-threatening illness need from you? How can you help him in his struggle to survive?

Too often we turn to medical experts for answers to those questions. Instead, we could turn to the real experts — the patients, themselves. Here are the stories of four such patients, each courageously waging a battle for survival. These patients share a need for honesty, empathy, and support. But they also share a more profound need to be heard and treated as unique human beings in unique situations. Their stories make an unstated plea: "If you want to know what we need, ask *us*."

Evelyn Bourgault Antil, RN, MS, former inservice instructor at Burbank Hospital, Fitchburg, Mass., discovered that she had breast cancer in 1972, just one year after becoming Service Committee Chairman with the Massachusetts Cancer Society. After a radical mastectomy, she returned to work, only to discover a lump in her other breast in 1974. The second breast changes were treated with chemotherapy and cobalt treatments. In 1975, she returned with widespread metastases.

At the time of this interview, Mrs. Antil was on chemo-

therapy. That treatment, the last available to her, failed. On February 24, 1976, Evelyn Bourgault Antil died.

'You know, it's almost as though my getting cancer was by design. I mean, we all ask ourselves, "Why me?" And my answer has been that, as a Reach to Recovery worker, now I can understand my patients better.

'I'd been following my own preachings about self-breast exams, and that's how I first discovered the lump. When I told the doctor, he didn't think it was anything. So, I didn't pursue it. After all, that's what I wanted to hear. And I think we nurses tend to say less to physicians about our physical problems anyway because we feel we're being overanxious or overdirective. It's a problem we've got to work to overcome.

'But one night watching T.V., I just happened to cross my arms over my chest. And this time there was no doubt about it—the lump was there. I had that sinking, sick feeling that, my God, it was there.

'I hurried back to my doctor. So, then it was rush, rush to get ready for biopsy—first a chest X-ray, then a metastatic series.

'I guess the thought of cancer was in the back of my mind. But while my mind was telling me one thing, my heart was telling me another—"No, it can't happen to me." It didn't really hit me until that metastatic series.

'When I asked the X-ray tech what she was doing, she said, "Well, your particular doctor orders these routinely to make sure there isn't any involvement in the bones. Because if there were, maybe he wouldn't do the surgery. Maybe he'd take another approach."

'She handled it well. But, oh, did it hit me hard! Because it made me think, "This could be the real thing."

'After the test results came back, my doctor told me I'd have to have a biopsy. He said, though, that "Nine times out of ten these things are benign." And his secretary said the same thing. In fact, everyone did. They were very careful to avoid that dread word — cancer. I knew why — because they truly hoped I didn't have it, because they wanted to encourage me.

'You know, it's funny. Before this happened I thought patients would resent the "nine-times-out-of-ten" kind of comment. I thought I'd turn around and say, "Yeah, that's easy for *you* to say." But I didn't. Because I needed those good wishes, people's prayers. I guess that just goes to prove that it doesn't matter so much *what* you say as *how* you say it.

'Still, no one was leveling with me. And, boy, I needed that

too. Because deep down I had the feeling that this was it. I think every patient in the same situation feels that way, unless he's denying very strongly — and I'm not sure anyone can deny so strongly that the thought doesn't at least cross his mind. So, I tried to prepare myself and my family for any outcome.

'Meanwhile, I was very fortunate in that a very dear friend of mine, Simone, was working on my floor when I went into the hospital. The day of the biopsy, she made a special request to prep me for surgery. As she was prepping me, I remembered this brownish discoloration on my breast. And, without thinking, I blurted out, "Simone, can't that be indicative of the real thing?"

'What a horrible question to ask her! I mean, it really put her on the spot. But Simone, bless her, came through. She hesitated a second and then said, "Yes, to my knowledge, it can."

'In that moment she helped me more than anyone else, more than all the good wishes and prayers. Because here, at last, was someone who would let me talk about it, let me get all my fears out — who wasn't trying to hush me up. Her telling me

'Deep down I had the feeling that this was it. I think every patient in the same situation feels that way, unless he's denying very strongly — and I'm not sure anyone can deny so strongly that the thought doesn't at least cross his mind.'

'You know, you really have to have lived a bit and suffered a bit before you can tune in to your patients. I can still remember my feelings then — the fear of metastasis, the old anxious mouth, the dried tongue that couldn't stop talking, the block I had against swallowing. Now when a patient says to me, "Look, I just can't eat today," I understand.'

the truth helped me face everything that was to come.

'Before the first biopsy, I signed the papers saying the doctors could do whatever was necessary. I knew that could mean a mastectomy if the biopsy was positive.

'When I woke up after surgery, the sense of the missing breast wasn't as alarming as seeing that Thiotepa had been added to my I.V. To me that said, "Cancer and spread." Because I knew that Thiotepa was one of those drugs they use in case any cancerous cells have escaped into the bloodstream during surgery. I think that's when my dread of I.V.s started. It wasn't the I.V. itself but rather its significance.

'Of course, the thought that my life was threatened loomed largest at first. But then came the need to help my family handle that knowledge. And finally the coping with the pain, the discomfort and the anxiety of it all.

'I guess my greatest emotional reaction was a subdued anger. Anger at myself for not having insisted on mammograms. Anger that I'd let denial rule my cognitive senses. Anger that I hadn't gone back to the doctor sooner (I'd had continuing doubts for 2 months after my first visit). And anger that I felt intimidated, that I hadn't wanted to appear to be a hypochondriac.

'In the next few weeks, I think I learned more about patients than I had in all my years as a nurse. You know, you really have to have lived a bit and suffered a bit before you can tune in to your patients. I can still remember my feelings then — the fear of metastasis, the old anxious mouth, the dried tongue that couldn't stop talking, the block I had against swallowing. Now when a patient says to me, "Look, I just can't eat today," I understand. I know it's because she's so full of anxiety. And I know not to push her. Because food isn't always that important to patients; sometimes they have other needs, emotional needs, that have to be met first.

'Anyhow, after the surgery, I had radiation therapy. And, as time went along, I began to feel much better. There I was, surviving after my life had been threatened. It was a marvelous feeling. I could go back to work; I was eating and drinking well; I was alive and living normally — at least for a while.

'But then, 2 years later, my other breast became swollen—red, hard—and the nipple was inverting . . . all the cardinal signs of cancer. I went back to my doctor. He didn't think it was anything to be concerned about. But this time I pressed for exams and more mammograms, Xerograms, and more thermograms — you know, the works.

'By that time, the lump had progressed to a stage where neither of us could deny it any longer. I started to have eruptions, papular eruptions — *peau d'orange,* as they call them . . . a very appropriate description because the skin actually looks granular and thick, like the skin of an orange. It was surfacing, for God's sake!

'My doctor did another biopsy. Only this time, I didn't sign a blanket surgical form. Instead I wrote right on the permit, "Do the biopsy only. If further surgery is indicated, I want to talk first with the doctor." You see, this time I wanted to deliberate about a mastectomy, to have some say in my fate. I felt as though the cancer was taking over my body. And I desperately needed to have some sense of control over what was happening to me.

'I think that's something nurses should encourage in patients, that control over their treatment. Sure, some patients are demanding a voice in their treatment. But not nearly enough. And I think it's up to us nurses to make sure they do — to make sure they ask questions and read every form they sign, or even to modify forms. I mean, isn't that what the Patients' Bill of Rights is all about? And who, other than nurses, are in a position to advocate that?

'Well, anyhow, the biopsy report came back positive. But it was a different kind of cancer than the other. My local doctor referred me to Peter Bent Brigham Hospital and the Sidney Farber Cancer Center in Boston. The doctors there felt that a mastectomy wasn't indicated — both because of the type of cancer and because of the extensive spread to the lymph glands. So, they decided on a bilateral oophorectomy and adrenalectomy, followed by radiation.

'Frankly, the thought that they'd treat the left side with radiation rather than a mastectomy came as a relief. I'd had cobalt treatments on the right breast, so I knew they weren't painful. And I'd had so much pain and discomfort and anxiety after the right mastectomy that I would've dreaded another one—the pain more than the disfigurement.

'The doctors did the oophorectomy and adrenalectomy in one sitting. But I wasn't too upset about it because I'd heard the story about a dear friend's sister, who hadn't been able to walk because of metastases to her bones. She'd had an adrenalectomy and after it was able to walk again. Her story encouraged me tremendously. I think it's important for nurses

'Now I know that we nurses should be more open with patients. I've found how much better I do knowing what I have to face and hearing about the alternative treatments. I know from experience that fear of the unknown is much greater than the fear of reality.'

to pass along encouraging anecdotes like that when a patient is down. They can be real morale boosters.

'After surgery, I started on radiation therapy and chemotherapy injections, which I dreaded because of the nausea and anorexia. I'd be nauseated the day before, the day of, and the day after each injection, which happens to a lot of patients. In fact, some have said they wonder if it's worth it — just to stay alive! Anyway, after 30 trips to the clinic for that, I was so hopeful of remission. Actually, I did quite well for a while — got back to work part-time, played golf, etc. But then, recurrence. The cancer ping-ponged back to the site of the 1972 mastectomy.

'I was really depressed when I was readmitted to the hospital. It seemed that no matter what the doctors did, the damn cancer would just spring up again. What helped most were the visits from the social worker, nurses, and doctors who'd become close friends during my other stay — and, of course, from my family and friends. I needed to have people there.

'As always, the great staff was forever encouraging about trying new approaches. First they removed the fluid from my right lung, which relieved me considerably. Then they tried new chemotherapeutic agents, which were very successful. After just a couple of treatments, the papules started flattening. To me that said, "If it's working on the outside, it's gotta be doing some good inside."

'Unfortunately, though, examination of the lung fluid showed metastasis to the lungs, which accounted for the fluid. The doctor who was to follow me on outpatient really leveled with me and helped me to take that awful news. So, I was put back on chemotherapy. I've been on it once a week for about 9 months.

'When I first went on this chemotherapy regime, by the way, I remembered the nausea from my other chemotherapy stint. So, a couple of weeks after I'd started on it, I complained to my nurse, Joyce, that I didn't see how I could play golf because I was nauseated so many days out of the week. She said, "But, Evelyn, you aren't *supposed* to be sick with these new meds!" And I said, "Well, nobody told *me* that." And, do you know, I haven't been sick since then! That really says a lot about the power of positive thinking and suggestion. You see how important it is to explain things to patients?

'That experience alone shows why I say it was almost by design, my getting cancer. Because now I'm so much more in tune with the "tears and laughter" — as Kahlil Gibran says — of my fellow man. I'd never choose to go through this experience again. But still, it's given me so much.

'Now, for instance, I know that we nurses should be more open with our patients. Why? Because I've found how much better *I* do knowing what I have to face and hearing about the alternative treatments. I know from experience that fear of the unknown is much greater than the fear of reality. In fact, I feel so strongly about honesty that I share everything — as gently as possible — with my husband and four children, as well as with relatives and dear friends and acquaintances. I just feel too much energy is dissipated in playing games.

'Of course, we all have different ways of coping. If someone doesn't want to know the truth about his condition and copes better that way, he has a right *not* to know too. I guess the point is that we nurses must try to "read" each patient and family — really listen to what they're saying *and* not saying — and then respond to the cues and clues we pick up.

'I've found too that it's important to share all your feelings and emotions, as well as information. Some of the other patients at the center have told me I'm good for their morale because I'm going all the time and always so optimistic. But just recently I had an injection that was unbelievably painful and I guess I panicked. I was scared, scared, scared because I thought a nerve had been hit. So, I really let it all hang out — crying, feeling very badly for myself. But something good came out of the experience.

'A fellow patient, whom I've become especially close to, was in the treatment room with me at the time. She's always seen Evelyn Antil as looking and doing so well, being so brave, etc. Yet there she saw me with all the fears and weaknesses that she has. So maybe now she doesn't feel so alone, so much less strong than others.

'Despite the moments of doubt like that, though, I'm living fully and loving every precious moment. Of course, I've had to give up my challenging job and abandon the two programs I'm proud to have started at Burbank Hospital — the hospital-based home health program and the inpatient mental health department. But I have plenty of leisure time to do so many other things — reading, visiting, volunteering for the local branch of Reach to Recovery, even lecturing sometimes. My oldest daughter has told me that she feels I'm getting too wrapped up in this cancer thing. Maybe she's right. But there's so much to tell and right now time seems so short.

'You see, I have so much to live for. But at the same time I'm not afraid of death. Two years ago, I realized I might be dying. And in a profound religious experience, I discovered that if I should die, it would be all right. I'd be leaving my good life behind. But I feel I've experienced more love and fulfillment in my years than many other people do in 80 or 90 years. So I'm revelling in my life now more than ever before—every day, hour, second, moment.'

Norwin Synnestvedt

Margot English (a pseudonym) is a 25-year-old editor for a major book publisher. She contracted Hodgkin's disease when she was 13. Because her parents refused to tell her, she didn't discover the nature of her illness until she was 18. After radiotherapy, she remained in remission for 5 years, followed by another course of radiotherapy. Then she suffered a relapse, which was treated with chemotherapy. Margot now has been in remission for 2 years.

'Maybe you won't understand why I don't want my name printed or to have people know I have Hodgkin's disease. But I'm adamant about it. Because my experience has been that, when people find out, they reject you. You can almost feel them drawing away. You know? It's hard to believe that kind of thing can happen in this day and age, but it does. People still have a horror about cancer.

'I remember one time at work, a woman had read a newspaper article about some town that'd had a rash of cancer. She started insisting that it was contagious and that *she* sure didn't want to be exposed to it. I thought, "Oh, lady, if you only knew!"

'I've also had friends find out and after a while, they just didn't get in touch anymore. I was even dating a med student and we were thinking about getting married. But in the end, he backed out because all he could see was himself taking care of an invalid for the rest of his life. He just couldn't handle it. In fact, he even made me feel guilty about having this thing, as though it were my fault. If a medical person can react that way, what can you expect from nonmedical people? If the people at work knew, I'm afraid I'd lose my job. And if people in my hometown found out, I'd become a cocktail party conversation piece.

'My parents know, obviously. My sister knows. And I've

told a few of my closest friends. But, for my own peace of mind, I keep it from everyone else. Even my brother doesn't know.

'Sometimes that means lying. Like, this morning I had an early appointment at the clinic for a check-up and my two roommates asked where I was going. I had to invent a plausible excuse. But most of the time it's just a matter of not telling. And I guess I find that easier than most people because I wasn't told for so long.

'In that respect, I'm much different from most Hodgkin's patients. Most know their diagnosis right away and have to cope with it *and* the treatments all at once. By the time I found out I had Hodgkin's, I'd been living with it for about 5 years. So, you know, I never felt the full impact of it. Sure, at first I was shaken when I read in medical books that the average life expectancy for Hodgkin's patients was only a few years. But when I thought about it later, there I was, a 5-year veteran and still going strong. So somehow I just didn't feel that "average" data applied to me.

'All those years, my parents had been taking me to cancer clinics for radiology treatments, telling me that I had a problem with my lymph glands, which was true. But it wasn't until I was 18 that I learned just how serious that problem was. A woman sitting next to me in one clinic asked if I had cancer. I gave her an emphatic, "No!" at the time. But she planted the seeds of suspicion. Then I finally decided that, yeah, I did have cancer.

'When I confronted my doctor with it, he admitted it. It must've been a tremendous relief for my parents, getting it out in the open, because they'd kept that awful secret to themselves for so long. I guess some people might resent their parents for not telling them. But I don't. Adolescence is a hard period anyhow. I don't think I could've handled it then. I would've gone crazy.

'When I found out the truth, I didn't go through the various stages you hear about — none of the bargaining or disbelief. I guess I did feel pretty angry — you know, "Why me?" But my main reaction was just like in the movies — that I only had a short time to live and that I was going to make the most of it. Everything became so important to me — the way things looked, how people reacted to me, everything. For several months, I just couldn't shake the thought of having cancer.

'After a while, though, I thought about it less often. I was

surviving, making it. I was in remission and it wasn't affecting my everyday life. So, you know, it just didn't seem that threatening. Occasionally I'd get very depressed about it. But it didn't drag me down on a day-to-day basis.

'But then, 3 years ago, I had a flare-up and had to go on chemotherapy. For the first time, I realized how deadly this disease was.

'Chemotherapy was ungodly. First of all, there was the nausea from the treatments. Believe me, it was like nothing you've ever experienced — constant, wracking vomiting every 15 minutes for 4 to 6 hours after each treatment. I'd vomit until I thought my insides would come out. It got to the point where just the sight of the needle or the thought of treatments could touch off the nausea.

'And it was a terribly lonely experience. Because no one could help me through it. It was just me and that drug, fighting it out. Unfortunately, people — even medical people — don't always understand what you're going through. I remember one time when a doctor, not my regular doctor, was trying to get the needle in for a treatment. He was having a lot of trouble and finally I starting sobbing, "I can't take it, I can't take it anymore." He told me, rather curtly, to stop making such a fuss. I exploded. I said, "Look, do you think I *enjoy* coming here for this, knowing that I'll walk out of here and vomit my guts out for the next few hours?"

'His response was: "Do you think you're the first person who's felt that way?"

'Well, obviously I wasn't the first. But right then I didn't care whether I was the first or the forty-thousandth. I was going through my own private hell. And the fact that other people had gone through it wasn't any consolation. I realize he couldn't ease the agony for me. But if he'd just held my hand and said, "Hey, it's going to be okay. I know it's hell now, but it's going to be okay." That's really what I needed. I mean, a nurse's or doctor's technical skills are important — I've got scars from poor injections and stains from chemical infiltrations to attest to that. But, aside from them, one of the single most important attributes for a nurse or doctor working with cancer patients is just one hell of a lot of sympathy and moral support.

'You see, during chemotherapy, every patient cares only about himself. Hearing a doctor — and it's usually doctors who're condescending, not nurses — hearing them say, "Oh,

'Chemotherapy was a terribly lonely experience. Because no one could help me through it. It was just me and that drug, fighting it out. Unfortunately, people — even medical people — don't always understand what you're going through.'

'Undoubtedly the most devastating side effect of my chemotherapy was losing my hair. That may sound ridiculous. But I don't think you realize how much your hair is a part of your identity until you lose it. When it falls out, it's like watching your body disintegrate before your eyes.'

stop it. I've heard all that before," only makes things worse. There's a fine line between feeling that it's okay to have certain fears because everyone has them and feeling that they're not important because everyone has gone through the same thing.

'Undoubtedly the most devastating side effect of my chemotherapy — even worse than the nausea — was losing my hair. That may sound ridiculous. But I don't think you realize how much your hair is a part of your identity until you lose it. When it falls out, it's like watching your body disintegrate before your eyes. You begin to realize just what this disease can do to you.

'The doctors had warned me that I'd lose my hair, of course. But I wasn't fully prepared for seeing clumps of it coming out in my hands. It really freaked me out. In fact, I wrote a passage in my journal at the time that goes something like, "Hair, *hair,* HAIR. Long hair, gone hair, far away and falling off, off, OFF. Disappearing. Sinking down. . . . " The passage goes on like that for three pages. It's the work of a mad person, really.

'Of course, I could wear a wig. But that interfered with my personal relationships. I was always looking in mirrors and windows to see if it was on straight. And whenever I'd go out with a man, I'd end up huddled as far from him as possible because I was afraid he'd touch my head and the wig would slip, or fall off.

'The only person who could really handle my feelings at that time was my sister. She was tremendous because she was so matter-of-fact about everything. For instance, I remember one time, my wig was getting pretty ratty but I was still wearing it because I hoped that within a couple of weeks I'd have enough hair back to get rid of the wig. Well, as we were shopping, my sister glanced at me and said, "Let's get you another wig" — another "Gladys," as we called it. I said, no, it was a waste of money. But she insisted because she said it'd make me feel better. So, we bought one more like my own hair. And I felt amazingly better.

'Even with her around to talk to, though, the fears and resentment about being discovered and about what this disease was doing to me got to be too much for me to handle. Finally, one of the nurses gave me the name of a psychologist. (Not a psychiatrist. I deliberately chose a psychologist because I didn't want an MD who'd know about Hodgkin's or who might have outdated information about it.) I can honestly say that that was one of the best things the nurses did for me. I went to the psychologist regularly for 6 months and then periodically for another 6 to 8 months. During our time together, I got out a lot of pent-up anger and resentment, and he helped me deal with it all.

'About this same time, my doctor also introduced me to Helen, another Hodgkin's patient at the center. Helen and I were different in many respects — she was older and had a husband and kids. But we had our feelings and reactions to chemotherapy in common. So, we became good friends.

'A few months after I met Helen, though, a dreadful thing happened — Helen began dying. She got a cord compression and eventually became paralyzed from the neck down. She lasted that way only a few months. But, God, it seemed like forever.

'Towards the end, I didn't know how to handle the situation. If I went to see Helen, I'd come away completely shaken; but if I stayed away, I'd feel guilty. Eventually I did stop seeing her. The guilt was a bit easier to cope with then the terror.

'That whole relationship was very painful for both of us. For Helen, because she was dying and my "health" seemed so unjust; for me, because I was seeing, for the first time, a fellow Hodgkin's patient fade away. Her death produced an irrational fear in me that I still can't lose, more than a year later. Whenever things begin going badly health-wise for me, I think I'm becoming like Helen — that I'll just fade away too.

'Despite that, though, I think the relationship was important for me. First of all, I needed to talk with someone who'd lost her hair and now had it growing back. But more than that, I needed to get out all my anger and hostility. I could direct it away from myself and focus it on her death. Her death really jolted me back into reality. And in spite of my fears of becoming like her, deep down I feel that I'll defeat the Hodgkin's before it defeats me. I'm not saying I'm better than Helen; it's just that I feel I have more psychic and physical energy than she did.

'Well, my chemotherapy finally ended eight months after I'd started. That was a day of rejoicing. You see, chemotherapy is one of those experiences that can't be described in rational language. I'd counted the days, treatments, hours until it would end. I still live in fear that I'll have to go through it again.

'I still worry about having a relapse sometimes — I don't think you ever forget about it totally. But now when I get depressed, I just call my doctor. He's been treating me for five years, so we've become as much friends as doctor-patient. Anyhow, I'll call him and say, "Hey, I'm really down." And he'll say, "Okay, let's talk about it." He's great.

'Unfortunately, a lot of doctors aren't that open or warm. They just don't seem to have the time or interest to get involved with their patients. I guess that's why I think nurses have to make an extra effort to give patients support. They have to take up the slack that the doctors leave.

'Nurses have got to be empathetic, concerned, and above all honest. Patients need a sense that the nurses care — and for most of us that means a hug, or hand-holding, or total sincerity and humanness. But none of that can take precedence over honesty. Naturally if nurses don't know the complete situation, they shouldn't offer inaccurate information. But if they do know, they shouldn't pretend they don't.

'You see, the only way any of us can decide how we want to live our lives is if we know what's happening to us. And with cancer patients, particularly the ones in the advanced stages, those decisions are, God, they're so important. Let's face it: sometimes they're all the patient has left.'

Mark Reinsberg, from Bethesda, Md., is a renal dialysis patient. Although he experienced minor kidney disturbances for several years, he maintained adequate renal function until 1974. At that time, though, he underwent a nearly fatal triple-bypass operation on his heart. Mr. Reinsberg survived the surgery, but his kidneys didn't. Today he must be dialyzed three times a week. He has retired from his former job as a speechwriter and now spends most of his time working around his family home.

'As you can imagine, being on dialysis is always a demanding experience. Not only do you have the physical ups and downs. You also have such a large chunk of your week eaten up at the dialysis center.

'I spend — and I guess I'm typical in this respect — I spend five hours a day, three days a week on the machine. That's about 15 hours a week. Plus maybe an hour to an hour-and-a-half while I'm being connected to the machine or disconnected. That makes it closer to 20 hours a week, which is approximately the equivalent of a part-time job.

'Naturally, it's physically exhausting. But more than that, it's psychologically exhausting — having to devote so much time to the simple act of surviving. You've got to deal with the experience as unemotionally as possible. For me, that's meant more or less regarding it as a part-time job. On days when the kids are home, I look at the clock and say, very cheerfully, "Well, time for me to go to work." I say to myself, well, it's my job to supply blood to keep this pump going for three shifts a week.

'I've also learned to regard the actual process of dialysis very clinically. Like most renal patients, when I first went on dialysis, I didn't pay much attention to the process. For so long I'd felt, God, just rotten — pain, no endurance, total lack of concentration. So, you know, I was just grateful that something was being done for me. But as I began to feel better, I also began to notice what a bloody business dialysis is — the gallons and gallons of human blood, mine and other people's. At first it's a pretty unnerving sight for a patient, seeing his life flow by him. I found it best to think of all that blood as so much red ink.

'In dialysis, a good day is almost miraculous. I've learned not to expect it. Sometimes the needle hurts and sometimes it doesn't. Sometimes I get cramps or nausea. Sometimes the machine malfunctions and I end up loaded with saline solution. Sometimes I'm able to lie back in my chair and feel as if I were in a fancy hotel barber shop. Other times, say when the access point on my arm (my fistula) shows signs of giving out, I worry about the possibility of more surgery. If I make it through my five hours without any major crisis or pain, I'm happy.

'I don't mean to imply that I'm always on pins and needles about what my reaction will be. Of course it gnaws at the back of my mind. But generally those five hours are plain boring. Sometimes I can carry on snatches of conversation with the patients next to me. But we may have nothing in common or they may want to sleep. If I feel alert enough, I can read. Or I can sleep. They take your blood pressure every half hour, but you learn to ignore that.

'Even though I usually do sleep for an hour to two, I feel a little bit uneasy about it. There are just too many things that could go wrong. Once in a while, for instance, patients get a leak in their coil. An amazing number are defective or get damaged in handling. Or if it's not the coil, something can go wrong with the line. A new therapist might clamp the wrong tube. Or, for whatever reason, your arm may get infiltrated

'There's an underground network of communications among patients — who's a good therapist and who isn't, which centers are good and which aren't, and so on. It's underground in that we rarely talk about it if a nurse or doctor — anyone in authority — is present. Why? Because most patients, being dependent on the dialysis centers, are afraid to antagonize the people who run them.'

and swell up. You could even pass out while you're sleeping and the therapist might not notice right away.

'Knowing how much can go wrong — and when your life depends on that machine, believe me, you make sure you know — knowing that, you pray you don't get an incompetent therapist who'll increase the risks. There's an underground network of communications among patients about that sort of thing — who's a good therapist and who isn't, which centers are good and which aren't, and so on. I don't mean that it's a furtive network — most of our conversations take place right in the treatment anteroom. But it's underground in that we rarely talk about it if a nurse or doctor — anyone in authority — is present. Why? Because most patients, being dependent on the dialysis centers, are afraid to antagonize the people that run them.

'Anyway, the exchange of information among patients is good in some ways. It's helpful to know, for example, which therapists are fumblers, which mess up fistulas or cause pain or forget clotting problems. That way, you can try to avoid the bad therapists — say, by changing your time slot or telling the social worker that you don't want a particular person.

'At the same time, though, an awful lot of misinformation gets spread through this grapevine. And in centers where the staff doesn't believe in open discussion of treatments, it can be a bit dangerous.

'At any rate, nearly every patient is all too aware of what can happen to him during dialysis. After all, they see it happening to other patients. For instance, at our center, which I consider better than average, someone passes out about once every two months. Sometimes it's from dehydration, sometimes from a cardiac condition or a malfunction of the machine. But the point is that, whatever the cause, seeing a patient go out of the center feet first is pretty unnerving. And it's particularly devastating if the center has a hush policy — where you simply don't ask about such things. Because that leaves you wide open to speculate about the ineptness of the technicians. Could they have prevented it? What're the chances it'll happen to you? It's one more worry.

'Usually we don't talk about that sort of feeling, though. There's an unstated taboo against discussing anything very personal — feelings, money. I once made the mistake of asking another patient how much money he got from Medicare. He told me, but I realized immediately it was the wrong thing to ask. For the most part, we keep our fears and problems to ourselves — as Thoreau said, living out our lives of quiet desperation.

'Dialysis is probably the most dramatic facet of renal care, or at least what the public thinks about. But the damnable thing about kidney disease is that it upsets every aspect of your life, particularly family life.

'First of all, you can't work. I know a couple of renal patients who do — a lawyer and a doctor. But they're rare. Most are like me — they simply don't have the time or energy. I've had to give up my job. Which means that my wife's had to take over the breadwinning.

'So, you see, we've had a complete reversal of roles. I'm no longer the decision-maker; I'm the house-husband. It's been only within the past few months that I've been able to assume even small household chores and bits of family management — balancing the checkbook and that sort of thing. Most of the household burden still falls on my wife, in addition to the burden of having to work and take care of the kids.

'Naturally all that's affected how we relate, even our sex lives. I haven't become impotent, as some dialysis patients have. But most of the time, one or the other of us is just plain too exhausted for sex. Fortunately we have an open enough relationship that we can talk about how that makes us feel. But can you imagine what happens to couples who can't talk about it? They must have tremendous psychological problems — feelings of rejection or resentment or worthlessness or whatever. And, of course, no one at the center discusses that with you unless you initiate the conversation, which isn't easy to do.

'How extensively dialysis affects a patient's sex life varies. But you know what I think is the most important factor? I think it's how the *spouse* is affected by the problem. If he or she is emotionally upset or resents having to take on all the work, the relationship will really suffer.

'In addition to the job and sex problems, my wife and I also have the diet problems to contend with at home. God, you begin by spending half your time just trying to figure out what you can eat that won't kill you. You see, they give you a diet that says, well, you can't have this and you can't have that or you'll die immediately. It scares the hell out of you.

'In time, of course, you learn to relax a little about it. The turning point for me came when I noticed that one fellow at my

first dialysis center always had the best hematocrit levels. Finally, one day I asked him, "Bill, how do you do it?" And he said, "Well, I eat what I want to eat, when I want to eat it." That's when I realized there weren't any absolutes. Now I pretty much eat what I want to eat — within reason, of course.

'I've been on dialysis now for almost a year. And I feel an awful lot better. I know there are still limitations. And I have less emotional reserves. But I feel halfway decent most of the time. There are even short periods where I forget there was ever anything wrong with me. Dialysis can do that. You don't really consider yourself sick. I mean, you're sick if you have the flu or the mumps, something like that. But kidney failure is something else — not quite illness, not quite health.

'In my time on dialysis, I've seen a lot of different dialysis centers — some good, some not so good. I try to decide what makes the difference. And I think it's their openness and the people who staff them. I feel most confident in the units that use more nurses — the smaller centers or teaching hospitals. You see, dialysis patients rarely see a doctor for an extended conference. Barring any crisis, it's usually a fleeting encounter each session to report any problems and check blood counts. So, the most important people in our lives are the ones running that machine. Most of the technicians are kind and dedicated. But they just lack the depth of experience and the medical knowledge of a nurse. I'm not suggesting that only nurses should run the machines — anyone can do that. What I'm suggesting is that they have more contact with the patients during dialysis.

'I'm also suggesting that nurses become more of a patient's advocate. They're in a unique position to do that because they're close to the patient — sometimes they see as much of him as the spouse! As I've said, too many patients can't — or are afraid to — articulate what they deeply feel. But a good nurse should be able to anticipate problems.

'For instance, the fistula. Every patient worries about how it looks. But nurses could lessen the psychological trauma by developing a strategy to minimize the scar by rotating the puncture sites. As it stands now, too often the technicians use whatever site is most convenient.

'Or, if the patient develops a problem with his fistula, the nurses should help him determine the best alternative. Doctors are too quick to recommend surgery because it's most convenient for them. And most patients aren't strong enough

'My wife and I have had a complete reversal of roles. I'm no longer the decision-maker; I'm the house-husband. It's been only within the past few months that I've been able to assume even small household chores and bits of family management. Naturally all that's affected how we relate, even our sex lives.'

to defend their own interests. I'm not saying nurses should defy doctors. But surely they could bring the patient's point of view to the doctor's attention so he'll at least consider it.

'Or how about the diet? Patients agonize over it for 6 months to 2 years before they discover that it's all relative; a good nurse could spare them the months of hysteria just by taking a few minutes in the beginning to explain that individual capacities differ. Maybe they could work with the dietitians to eliminate those dogmatic diets and instead hand out a general list of no-no's. Whatever, I think they should be more of a normalizing voice.

'Maybe, too, it would help to get a patient profile from the family so you'll know what problems to anticipate with that patient. And talk with the family in a noncrisis situation to discover *their* problems.

'Face it — the family won't presume to call you to ask something as mundane as, say, "Well, how should I handle him when he comes home from dialysis and just sits and stares at the ceiling?" They think you're too busy to discuss things like that. They probably won't even open up if you approach them in a hurried moment. But maybe if you called on a slow day and said, "I'm calling because it's a quiet period and I just thought we could chat about any problems your husband (or wife) is having." That could lead to a tremendous discussion. I realize that you've got to retain your clinical detachment to function in this field. But I think you can have personal contact with a patient and his family without becoming socially or personally involved.

'Finally, I think someone's got to make a concerted effort to take the patient out of the holding pattern and get him back on the road to a productive life. The more a patient is encouraged to do, and does, the more he will do. I've found that myself. But when he takes those first faltering steps back to life, he needs a tremendous amount of hand-holding. I think nurses could give considerable help there. Sometimes just a little of your encouragement could make the difference between a patient giving up and waiting for death . . . and daring, hoping, to live again.'

Angela Cavagnaro discovered a lump in her lower abdomen in 1972. For some reason, the biopsy report came back "Benign." When another lump developed and was biopsied, however, the

report came back "Malignant melanoma." Further studies showed that the cancer had metastasized to the lungs, bones, and brain. Ms. Cavagnaro has been on chemotherapy for the past four years.

'From the very beginning, we've all talked openly about the cancer — me, my doctor, my husband, my family. It just happened that way because, when the doctor called with the second biopsy report, everyone was right there. It seemed senseless to try to hide it — I'm not sure I could've anyhow. And I'm glad for that. Because everyone — my husband, my children — has been such a help.

'The only exception we've made to total honesty's been with our youngest child. She was only 8 at the time, and we were afraid that, if we told her that I had cancer, she'd repeat it at school and some kid might say, "That means your mother's going to die." We didn't want her to get any false ideas, but we didn't want to lie either. So, we told her that I had a tumor and was very sick. It's only been in the past couple of months that I've used the word cancer with her. But she's 12 now, so I think she can handle it better.

'The one important person missing when that call came was my mother. She was on vacation. I knew it was going to be difficult to tell her when she came back, but I knew too that I'd have to. I've never been able to keep anything from her.

'Well, all the way out to the airport, I kept wondering: How am I going to tell her? What's she going to say? Will she, will either of us, break down? When I met her at the gate, I kissed her and asked all about her trip. But I didn't say anything about the biopsy because I wanted to wait 'til we were alone. When we got in the car and started driving, I took a deep breath and finally forced out, "Mom, the report came back from the doctor. The tumor was malignant."

'She didn't say anything for a minute. And then, without taking her eyes off the road, she said one line: "Honey, none of us goes before our time."

'I'll never forget those words. It was the best thing she could've said. Because it made me realize that, no matter what happened, it'd be all right. Even if I wasn't cured, it would be all right. That's the attitude I've kept with me all through therapy. It and my religious faith have sustained me through some pretty rough times.

'I've had the usual side effects from treatment: The skin problems from radiation and the nausea and hair loss from chemotherapy. Right now my hair's thin because it's just growing back in. But I wear it this way openly. I just don't see much point in hiding it.

'Anyway, the side effects seem to come and go. But I've also had some side effects from the brain tumor. For one thing, I've lost the peripheral vision in my left eye. For a while there, I was always running into things when I'd turn left. But I've learned to compensate for that by looking left when I turn. The only thing really that I can't do because of my vision is drive. But then, I've got family and friends who'll drive me around. So that's not much of a handicap.

'Another side effect is that I forget things sometimes. For a while in the hospital, I was completely out of it. I didn't know where I was or why. It was awful. But I'm a lot better now. The other day my doctor asked me if I sometimes go into a room and forget why I'm there. I said, "Yes, don't you?" I mean, everyone's a little forgetful. So this occasional memory loss doesn't seem so bad.

'I'm not saying there haven't been bad times. There have. But throughout it all, my husband's given me tremendous strength. One of the biggest helps is that he's always come into the treatment and examination rooms with me, to give me support. From what I hear, that's pretty unusual. But since he's in sales and can make his own work time, he's had the time to spend with me in the clinic. I must say that having him there's made treatment easier for me, especially in the beginning when it was all new and frightening. In fact, I think every patient would be better off if they could have a relative or someone close with them during therapy.

'My husband's become a real pro on my case, writing down everything the doctors've told us and discussing it with them. That's another benefit of having him there: We both know exactly where we stand — there's no deception and no confusion over whether the doctor said such-and-such or not.

'Now that my treatments are becoming more time-consuming and I'm more accustomed to them, my husband doesn't come as often; I don't feel he should take that much time away from work. So now I pretty much depend on friends to get me to and from the clinic. They've been great in every way, even in talking over everything. Oh, yes, we're very open about it. But we can afford to be, because we don't talk about it often. I couldn't bear it if we dwelled on it.

'Even though my husband's not coming to the clinic much

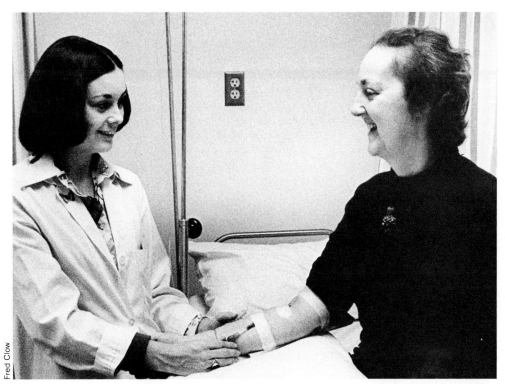

Fred Clow

anymore, he and I still discuss my case. Of course, we try to protect each other from unnecessary worries, like the medical expenses. But then I think there's a big difference between being open and being brutal. Let me give you an example.

'One afternoon I was sitting in the examination room waiting for my doctor, when a new doctor — a woman doctor — came striding in with my chart. She'd never seen me before, you understand; I have a regular doctor. But she studied my chart for a few minutes and then said to me, "Do you know why you're here?" I said, yes, of course I did — I had a brain tumor that the doctors wanted to examine for possible surgery. I said that they'd looked at it and found it was small, so they weren't going to operate.

'"Well," she snapped, "yes, you have a brain tumor. But it isn't small; it's deep and very large." And she walked out.

'Naturally I was terribly upset. In fact, I was shaking by the time my own doctor finally arrived. When I told him about it, he said to just ignore the other doctor. He said she didn't know my particular case the way he did, that he was the only one qualified to talk about it.

'Well, when I thought that over, I felt better. But you can

'I've had the usual side effects from treatment: The skin problems from radiation and the nausea and hair loss from chemotherapy. Right now my hair's thin because it's just growing back in. But I wear it this way openly. I just don't see much point in hiding it.'

imagine the scare that other doctor'd given me. I don't know why she said what she did. Maybe she'd had a bad day. Or maybe she'd looked at the wrong chart. Whatever the reason, she should've kept quiet or talked to my doctor first. Her kind of approach really does more harm than good. It's what I call brutality, not honesty.

'Now that I think about it, I had a similar frightening experience — but that one was my own fault. I'd noticed an article in one of the women's magazines — *Ladies Home Journal* or something — about cancer. Well, naturally I was interested.

'Actually it really didn't upset me too much until I hit the last line: "Melanoma (which is what I have) is the most deadly kind of cancer." I felt numb. For the rest of the week, that phrase kept running through my mind: Melanoma is the most deadly kind of cancer.

'Finally, at my next clinic appointment, I got up enough nerve to ask my doctor if that was true. He said, "Look, each patient reacts differently to this disease. You're an individual case. Knowing your case and reading about this disease is *our* job. It isn't *your* job. Your job is to be the patient."

'Well, ever since then I haven't read any more cancer articles, unless I can tell from the headlines that they're going to be optimistic. Otherwise, I know I'll just get depressed. If I want to know anything, I ask someone — usually a doctor, but sometimes the nurses, especially if the doctor's busy. If the nurses know, they generally tell me. But if not, they'll tell me to ask my doctor.

'That's one of the things I think's so fantastic about the nurses here — their honesty with everyone. In fact, I can't say enough good things about them. They're always so positive and cheerful. I've been coming here almost 4 years and, in all that time, never has a nurse upset me. They're very special.

'The way this clinic operates, it's almost like a family. Everyone seems to know everyone else. And they're always asking about other patients. I really appreciate that family feeling. Because when you're going through this kind of thing, you really need support. Not sympathy — *support*. There's a big difference, you know.

'Maybe that distinction doesn't sound so important to you. But it is to me because I'm going to need a lot of support. You see, my doctor's told me that I'll be on chemotherapy for the rest of my life. That might sound pretty awful to you. But I know that's the way it has to be.'

How do you view death?

WHAT DOES DEATH mean to *you*? To some people, it's the "grand perhaps." To others, it's the "poor man's doctor." To still others, it's punishment . . . relief . . . unfair . . . the grand leveler . . . merciful . . . eternal sleep . . . terrifying . . . a delightful hiding-place for weary men.

To some, death is the "new pornography" — a subject hidden from today's children and not discussed openly among adults, even professionals. Indeed, few among us like to think about the subject. And yet, nurses in particular, must. As a comforting companion to people on their way to face death, nurses are apt to witness death more often than almost any group — except perhaps soldiers in wartime.

To help you understand more about the subject, we have constructed a research questionnaire, which poses questions that aren't always easy to answer.

The questionnaire, designed under the direction of science editor David Popoff, has no right and wrong answers. The 70 questions will take only about 15 to 20 minutes to answer.

To make the best use of this questionnaire, record on a piece of paper the number of the answers that most closely match your views. Record only one answer to each question and always answer honestly.

When you have finished, read over your answers. They may help you clarify some of your thinking about death and dying — perhaps even arrive at a more mature, more comfortable perspective on it.

Once you have studied your own responses, you may want to compare them with the responses of more than 15,000 nurses who have already taken this questionnaire (Chapter 13). This comparison may also help you modify or strengthen your views on that mysterious but human process — death.

1. In your current work, how often do you deal with dying patients?
☐ 1. Usually every day
☐ 2. About once a week
☐ 3. Two or three times a month
☐ 4. About once a month
☐ 5. Once every 2 or 3 months
☐ 6. From one to five times a year
☐ 7. Almost never
☐ 8. Never

How often has caring for an incurable, terminally ill patient made you feel:

2. Discouraged?
☐ 1. Almost always
☐ 2. Occasionally
☐ 3. Seldom
☐ 4. Never

3. Depressed?
☐ 1. Almost always
☐ 2. Occasionally
☐ 3. Seldom
☐ 4. Never

4. Angry?
- ☐ 1. Almost always
- ☐ 2. Occasionally
- ☐ 3. Seldom
- ☐ 4. Never

5. Satisfied and fulfilled?
- ☐ 1. Almost always
- ☐ 2. Occasionally
- ☐ 3. Seldom
- ☐ 4. Never

Some nurses find it extremely difficult to cope with their own feelings when they have to care for certain kinds of dying patients. Assuming you were assigned to care for the following kinds of dying patients today, and assuming that their prognoses and symptoms were comparable, how would you feel?

6. A newborn infant?
- ☐ 1. Wouldn't mind
- ☐ 2. Somewhat uncomfortable
- ☐ 3. Very uncomfortable
- ☐ 4. Unable to cope

7. A young child?
- ☐ 1. Wouldn't mind
- ☐ 2. Somewhat uncomfortable
- ☐ 3. Very uncomfortable
- ☐ 4. Unable to cope

8. An adolescent?
- ☐ 1. Wouldn't mind
- ☐ 2. Somewhat uncomfortable
- ☐ 3. Very uncomfortable
- ☐ 4. Unable to cope

9. A young adult?
- ☐ 1. Wouldn't mind
- ☐ 2. Somewhat uncomfortable
- ☐ 3. Very uncomfortable
- ☐ 4. Unable to cope

10. A mother with young children at home?
☐ 1. Wouldn't mind
☐ 2. Somewhat uncomfortable
☐ 3. Very uncomfortable
☐ 4. Unable to cope

11. A father with a young family?
☐ 1. Wouldn't mind
☐ 2. Somewhat uncomfortable
☐ 3. Very uncomfortable
☐ 4. Unable to cope

12. A middle-aged person?
☐ 1. Wouldn't mind
☐ 2. Somewhat uncomfortable
☐ 3. Very uncomfortable
☐ 4. Unable to cope

13. An elderly person?
☐ 1. Wouldn't mind
☐ 2. Somewhat uncomfortable
☐ 3. Very uncomfortable
☐ 4. Unable to cope

14. A very old person?
☐ 1. Wouldn't mind
☐ 2. Somewhat uncomfortable
☐ 3. Very uncomfortable
☐ 4. Unable to cope

15. In general, how would you rate the requests for nursing care of most terminally ill patients as compared to that of other seriously ill patients?
☐ 1. Care of terminally ill patients is much more time-consuming.
☐ 2. Somewhat more time-consuming
☐ 3. About the same
☐ 4. Somewhat less time-consuming
☐ 5. Much less time-consuming

16. Based on your own observations, how would you rate the care and attention given by most nurses to dying patients?
- ☐ 1. Most nurses go out of their way to give extra care and comfort to dying patients.
- ☐ 2. Most nurses treat dying patients as well as they treat their other patients.
- ☐ 3. Most nurses avoid contact with dying patients, sometimes to the point of ignoring their call lights.

17. Have you ever received strength and support from a dying patient?
- ☐ 1. Yes
- ☐ 2. No

18. Have you ever assisted in an abortion procedure?
- ☐ 1. Yes
- ☐ 2. No

19. Have you ever refused to care for an abortion patient?
- ☐ 1. Yes, preoperatively only
- ☐ 2. Yes, postoperatively only
- ☐ 3. Yes, preoperatively and postoperatively
- ☐ 4. No
- ☐ 5. Never assigned to care for one

20. Have you ever had an abortion?
- ☐ 1. Yes
- ☐ 2. No

21. In your opinion, does a fetus have any rights — morally, legally, or otherwise?
- ☐ 1. Yes, from the moment of conception
- ☐ 2. Yes, from the time it might become viable outside the womb
- ☐ 3. No, such rights begin at birth

Do you approve or disapprove of each of the following reasons for abortion?

22. The woman and her husband do not want any more children.
- ☐ 1. Approve
- ☐ 2. Disapprove

23. The woman and her husband cannot afford any more children.
☐ 1. Approve
☐ 2. Disapprove

24. The woman is not married.
☐ 1. Approve
☐ 2. Disapprove

25. The woman has good reason to believe that the child would be deformed.
☐ 1. Approve
☐ 2. Disapprove

26. The woman had been raped.
☐ 1. Approve
☐ 2. Disapprove

27. Pregnancy would seriously endanger the woman's life.
☐ 1. Approve
☐ 2. Disapprove

28. In some hospitals, newborns with gross abnormalities are deliberately allowed to die when there is no possibility of any meaningful existence. Are you in favor of or against this practice?
☐ 1. In favor
☐ 2. Mixed feelings, slightly in favor
☐ 3. Mixed feelings, slightly against
☐ 4. Against

29. What are your feelings about capital punishment?
☐ 1. In favor
☐ 2. Mixed feelings, slightly in favor
☐ 3. Mixed feelings, slightly against
☐ 4. Against

30. When should a patient with a terminal illness be told that he is dying?

☐ 1. As soon as possible after the diagnosis is certain.

☐ 2. The news should be broken to the patient slowly over an extended period of time as the illness progresses.

☐ 3. A patient should be told only when in the last stages of dying and death is imminent.

☐ 4. A patient should never be told that he is dying, only that he has a serious illness.

☐ 5. Only when he asks.

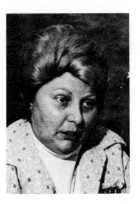

31. When a terminally ill patient brings up the topic of his death or dying, what is your honest inner reaction?

☐ 1. It makes me feel anxious and uncomfortable.

☐ 2. It makes me feel somewhat uncomfortable.

☐ 3. I feel somewhat relieved that the patient has brought up the topic.

☐ 4. I have never been involved in such a situation.

32. When a patient who has a terminal illness bluntly asks you if he is dying and his physician does not want the patient to know, what do you usually do?

☐ 1. Avoid the question and distract the patient in some way.

☐ 2. Reassure the patient that he is not dying, just ill.

☐ 3. Tell the patient that the question can be answered only by his physician and that you are not in a position to tell him.

☐ 4. Ask the patient why he brought up the question. Try to get him to talk about his feelings, and sit and listen to what he has to say.

☐ 5. Say you don't know.

☐ 6. Tell him the truth.

33. When physicians have refused to tell your patients that they were dying, how many of these patients nevertheless clearly knew of and referred to their impending death?

☐ 1. Very few, less that 10%

☐ 2. A small proportion, up to 25%

☐ 3. About half

☐ 4. A large proportion, up to 75%

☐ 5. A very large proportion, up to 90%

☐ 6. Every one, without exception

☐ 7. Have not cared for enough dying patients to estimate

34. In your own experience, how many terminally ill patients continued to deny, until the very end, that they would die?

☐ 1. Very few, less than 10%
☐ 2. A small proportion, up to 25%
☐ 3. About half
☐ 4. A large proportion, up to 75%
☐ 5. A very large proportion, up to 90%
☐ 6. Every one, without exception
☐ 7. Have not cared for enough dying patients to estimate

35. When is it usually more difficult to care for a terminally ill patient?
☐ 1. When the patient has been told he is dying
☐ 2. When the patient has not been told he is dying

36. When the family of a dying patient comes to you, how difficult is it for you to deal with them?
☐ 1. Usually very difficult
☐ 2. Difficult with some but not with others
☐ 3. Usually not difficult

37. Do you believe hospitals should have a separate department with a specially trained staff for the caring of terminally ill patients?
☐ 1. Yes
☐ 2. No

38. If a terminally ill patient does not want any life-sustaining efforts in his last stages of dying but his family insists that everything possible be done to prolong his life, whose desires do you believe should take priority?
☐ 1. The patient's
☐ 2. The family's

39. Sally, a nurse, has two terminally ill patients in her ward. She spends a great amount of time looking after and talking to these two patients. Her supervisor notices this and one day admonishes Sally, saying she is not providing equal care for her other patients. Do you think that Sally is right in giving priority to the care of dying patients?
☐ 1. Yes
☐ 2. No

What are your feelings about the following:

40. Withholding all life-sustaining treatment for dying patients who don't want it?
☐ 1. In favor
☐ 2. Mixed feelings, slightly in favor
☐ 3. Mixed feelings, slightly against
☐ 4. Against

41. Mercy killing or active euthanasia for dying patients who request it?
☐ 1. In favor
☐ 2. Mixed feelings, slightly in favor
☐ 3. Mixed feelings, slightly against
☐ 4. Against

42. Maintaining terminally ill patients by extraordinary means in order to study their disease?
☐ 1. In favor
☐ 2. Mixed feelings, slightly in favor
☐ 3. Mixed feelings, slightly against
☐ 4. Against

43. Do you believe that if a terminally ill patient is suffering beyond endurance and pleads for an end to his life, he should be given the means to do so?
☐ 1. Yes
☐ 2. It depends on the patient and on the circumstances
☐ 3. No

44. Have you ever knowingly helped hasten the death of a terminally ill patient?
☐ 1. No, never
☐ 2. Yes, once
☐ 3. Yes, several times, or more

45. Have any of the doctors or nurses you work with ever hastened the death of terminally ill patients?
☐ 1. Yes
☐ 2. No

46. Have any of the doctors or nurses you work with ever *intentionally* caused the death of a terminally ill patient?
☐ 1. Yes
☐ 2. No

47. What is your predominant feeling about having to care for the body of a patient after death?
☐ 1. Fear
☐ 2. Distaste
☐ 3. Acceptance of necessity of this task
☐ 4. No special feeling

48. Do you feel you have come to terms with your own fear of your own death?
☐ 1. Yes
☐ 2. To a great extent, yes
☐ 3. Only in part
☐ 4. No

49. Whose death produced the most profound effect on your attitude toward death and dying?
☐ 1. Grandparent
☐ 2. Parent
☐ 3. Brother or sister
☐ 4. Spouse
☐ 5. Son or daughter
☐ 6. Friend
☐ 7. Patient
☐ 8. Never had such an experience
☐ 9. Other (please specify) _____

50. What does death mean to you?
☐ 1. Reincarnation
☐ 2. Being with God
☐ 3. An ending of earthly life but with the continued individual existence of the soul
☐ 4. A joining of the soul with a universal consciousness
☐ 5. A kind of endless sleep
☐ 6. The end of all experiences; a total and irreversible blotting out of existence
☐ 7. Something other than the above (please specify) _____

51. What has had the *greatest* influence in shaping your present attitudes toward death and dying?
☐ 1. Religious teachings
☐ 2. Reading certain books and articles about death and dying
☐ 3. Conversation with terminally ill patients
☐ 4. Coping with the death of someone close
☐ 5. Introspection about my own death
☐ 6. Other (please specify) _____

52. In learning how to deal with the emotional and psychological problems of dying patients and their families, what has been your one best source of helpful advice and information?
☐ 1. Classes at nursing school
☐ 2. Books and magazine articles
☐ 3. An experienced, helpful staff member
☐ 4. Staff discussions
☐ 5. Working and talking with dying patients and learning from them
☐ 6. Seminars or workshops on death and dying
☐ 7. Other (please specify) _____

53. How confident do you feel in your ability to provide *technical* care to terminally ill patients?
☐ 1. Not at all confident
☐ 2. Slightly confident
☐ 3. Mostly confident
☐ 4. Very confident

54. How confident do you feel about your ability to manage the *psychological* needs of terminally ill patients?
☐ 1. Not at all confident
☐ 2. Slightly confident
☐ 3. Mostly confident
☐ 4. Very confident

55. How confident do you feel about your nursing abilities in general?
☐ 1. Not at all confident
☐ 2. Slightly confident
☐ 3. Mostly confident
☐ 4. Very confident

56. Have you ever been in a situation where you were told or felt certain that you might die in a relatively short period of time?
☐ 1. Yes
☐ 2. No

57. Have you ever thought seriously of committing suicide for any reason?
☐ 1. Yes, many times
☐ 2. Yes, a few times
☐ 3. No, never

58. If you were to commit suicide, what reason would be the most likely to cause you to do so?
☐ 1. Loneliness
☐ 2. Grief at the death of a loved one
☐ 3. Being rejected by someone you love deeply
☐ 4. Fear of insanity
☐ 5. Intractable pain and suffering
☐ 6. Terminal illness
☐ 7. Failure or disgrace
☐ 8. Depression and general unhappiness
☐ 9. Generally overwhelmed with problems
☐10. Very unlikely to commit suicide for any reason

59. How would you rate your views and beliefs in general?
☐ 1. Very conservative
☐ 2. Somewhat conservative
☐ 3. Moderate
☐ 4. Somewhat liberal
☐ 5. Very liberal

60. In general, how religious would you say you are?
☐ 1. Very religious
☐ 2. Moderately religious
☐ 3. Slightly religious
☐ 4. Not at all religious
☐ 5. Anti-religious

61. What is your religious denomination?
☐ 1. Protestant
☐ 2. Roman Catholic
☐ 3. Jewish
☐ 4. Other (please specify) _____
☐ 5. None

62. How often do you attend church or religious services?

☐ 1. Never
☐ 2. Occasionally
☐ 3. Frequently
☐ 4. Very frequently

63. What is your present marital status?

☐ 1. Single, never married
☐ 2. Married
☐ 3. Separated
☐ 4. Divorced
☐ 5. Widowed

64. What is your sex?

☐ 1. Female
☐ 2. Male

65. What is your age?

☐ 1. From 17 to 22
☐ 2. From 23 to 28
☐ 3. From 29 to 34
☐ 4. From 35 to 39
☐ 5. From 40 to 49
☐ 6. Fifty or over

66. What area do you presently in?

☐ 1. New England
☐ 2. Middle Atlantic states
☐ 3. South
☐ 4. Midwest
☐ 5. Southwest and Mountain states
☐ 6. West
☐ 7. Canada
☐ 8. Other

67. What level of nursing education have you completed?

☐ 1. Student nurse
☐ 2. Licensed practical nurse
☐ 3. Associate degree
☐ 4. Diploma (RN)
☐ 5. Baccalaureate degree
☐ 6. Master's degree
☐ 7. Doctorate

68. What is the highest nursing position you have attained?
- ☐ 1. Staff nurse
- ☐ 2. Team leader
- ☐ 3. Assistant head nurse
- ☐ 4. Head nurse
- ☐ 5. Supervisor
- ☐ 6. Nursing administrator
- ☐ 7. Other

69. Where do you now work?
- ☐ 1. Hospital, more than 200 beds
- ☐ 2. Hospital, less than 200 beds
- ☐ 3. Nursing home or ECF
- ☐ 4. Nursing school or university
- ☐ 5. School nurse
- ☐ 6. Industry
- ☐ 7. Community
- ☐ 8. Student nurse
- ☐ 9. Other

70. What is your area of specialty?
- ☐ 1. Medical/Surgical
- ☐ 2. ICU/CCU
- ☐ 3. Geriatrics
- ☐ 4. Emergency
- ☐ 5. Obstetrics/Gynecology
- ☐ 6. Pediatrics
- ☐ 7. Psychiatric
- ☐ 8. Hospital Administration
- ☐ 9. Other

How do others view death?

WHAT EMOTIONAL and psychological stresses do nurses experience from repeated contact with dying patients? What kinds of dying patients are most difficult to care for, and why? What do nurses feel about "hastening" the death of terminally ill patients?

The 15,430 responses to our questionnaire indicated that most nurses felt stimulated to examine more deeply their true feelings about what is, for most, an unpleasant subject. "Your questionnaire," one nurse wrote, "made me look into myself to see how I really feel about the various aspects of death. Thanks for giving me insight into my own feelings."

One nurse wrote that the questions "made it easier to examine my own feelings," but another found the questionnaire "most difficult to answer. As you can see, I changed many answers, sometimes many times." Difficult or not, respondents went out of their way to answer the questions as completely and honestly as possible. One could not sleep because of the questionnaire: "Please excuse my messy scribbling. It's 2:30 a.m. and I just had to get out of bed and add my personal feelings to the quiz. It'll be very interesting to see what the others feel."

The responses included: one school's entire class of nursing

TABLE 1 — A breakdown of respondents

Area of specialty		Region of residence	
Medical/surgical	34%	New England	8%
ICU/CCU	15	Middle Atlantic	22
Geriatrics	9	South	11
Pediatrics	7	Midwest	32
Emergency	5	Southwest and Mountain	7
Ob/Gyn	5	West	11
Psychiatric	4	Canada	8
Hospital administration	2	Other	1
Other	19		

Place of work		Religion	
		Protestant	51%
Hospital, more than 200 beds	47%	Roman Catholic	35
Hospital, less than 200 beds	20	Jewish	2
Nursing home or ECF	8	Other	6
Nursing school or university	6	None	6
School nurse	1		
Industry	1	Frequency of church attendance	
Community	3	Very frequent	23%
Student nurse	3	Frequent	26
Other	11	Occasional	38
		Never	13

Age		Self-rating of religiosity	
From 17 to 22	11%	Very religious	12%
23 to 28	36	Moderately religious	55
29 to 34	20	Slightly religious	23
35 to 39	9	Not at all religious	9
40 to 49	14	Anti-religious	1
50 and over	10		

Level of nursing education completed		Self-rating of general views and beliefs	
Student nurse	3%	Very conservative	4%
LPN	13	Somewhat conservative	21
Associate degree	9	Moderate	35
Diploma (RN)	48	Somewhat liberal	33
Baccalaureate degree	22	Very liberal	7
Master's degree	5		
Doctorate	0.1	Sex	
		Female	96%
		Male	4

Highest nursing position attained		Marital status	
Staff nurse	17%	Single, never married	29%
Team leader	22	Married	61
Asst. head nurse	11	Separated	2
Head nurse	17	Divorced	6
Supervisor	13	Widowed	2
Nursing administrator	6		
Other	14		

students . . . 14 participants in a hospital workshop "to stimulate self-appraisal" . . . an entire critical care unit in Maine. A head nurse said, "I wanted to share and explore responses with my own staff. We thought that when the results are published, we might see ourselves individually and collectively . . . . "

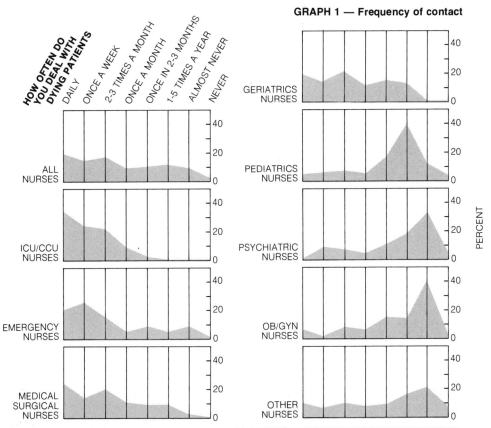

GRAPH 1 — Frequency of contact

Taking a look at Table 1, you can tell that our "typical" respondent was a 26-year-old midwestern diplomate who is a team leader in medical-surgical nursing. She's a married Protestant who attends church occasionally and considers herself moderately religious. She rates her views and beliefs as moderate. Of course, each respondent was unique, with special opinions. And that's what made the analysis of results fascinating.

As you'd expect, how often nurses deal with dying patients depends largely on where they practice.

The highest contact with dying patients occurs in ICU/CCU, emergency, medical/surgical, and geriatrics, in that order. The lowest contact with dying patients occurs in Ob/Gyn, psychiatry, and pediatrics (see Graph 1 for full details).

Frequency of contact with death

What nurses say about emotional reactions to death

"I get angry at the thought of a meaningful life going out too soon."
—Respondent #7872

"Caring for a dying patient has never made me angry, but when a person is brought into the E.R. already dead — like when a 6-year-old boy came in last summer after having been run over by a truck at 11 p.m. — anger is sometimes my primary emotion. In other words, if the *cause* of the death is unreasonable, the death angers me much more than the process of dying."
—Respondent #8688

"My anger is usually misdirected. I get angry at the patient for being so demanding, at the family for not understanding, at the doctor for allowing him to suffer, and at my co-workers for being uncaring. I suspect the real object of my anger is my own inability to deal with these and other problems at times."
—Respondent #9305

TABLE 2 — How often has caring for an incurable, terminally ill patient made you feel discouraged, depressed, or angry? (Q.2, Q.3, and Q.4)

	Discouraged	Depressed	Angry
Almost always	19%	21%	6%
Occasionally	62	58	41
Seldom	16	18	32
Never	3	3	21

The uninvolved nurses are more likely to become discouraged and depressed when they come into contact with a dying patient, and are less certain of their ability to provide technical care and to manage the psychological needs of terminally ill patients. However, when it comes to dealing with the fear of *one's own death,* we found little difference between nurses who have frequent contact with dying patients and those with little contact. Regardless of how much contact they have with dying patients, about one-half of all respondents have come to terms with their own death to a great extent, one-third only in part, and only about one-eighth have not yet done so.

Male nurses take care of dying patients just as frequently as female nurses. Young nurses tend to take care of dying patients more frequently than do older nurses: 40% of the nurses under age 28 care for dying patients at least once a week, compared to 25% of the nurses 40 or over. This shift may be due to higher concentrations of younger nurses in ICU/CCU, and of older nurses in administration.

Some 70% of nurses who provide *daily* care for dying patients work in large hospitals. In small hospitals and in nursing homes or extended care facilities, nurses are much less likely to be in daily contact with dying patients and, in fact, are most likely to see dying patients from one to three times a month. Though most nurses who deal daily with dying patients work in large hospitals, they do not always have to face the most difficult cases, at least in terms of personal involvement. Patients in small hospitals seldom are strangers to the nurses: they all live in the same town and may even be friends and neighbors.

Emotional reactions

Very few nurses escape being depressed and discouraged by terminal illness (see Table 2).

As one respondent explained, "Initial contact with dying persons always precipitates some feelings of discouragement, depression and anger, but I'm usually able to work these

TABLE 3 — How often has caring for an incurable, terminally ill patient made you feel satisfied and fulfilled? (Q. 5)
Have you ever received strength and support from a dying patient? (Q. 17)

Almost always	......17%	*Yes*	......70%
Occasionally	36	*No*	30
Seldom	27		
Never	20		

feelings through.'' Several wrote that *saddened* is a better word to describe their feelings.

Our cross-analysis showed: The more often a nurse becomes *angry* in this situation, the more likely she is to become discouraged and depressed. But not getting angry does not keep depression away; more than half of the nurses who never get angry do become discouraged and depressed at least occasionally. Young nurses between ages 17 and 22 show the greatest tendency to almost always become angry (12%), depressed (31%) and discouraged (26%). Male nurses, on the other hand, are the *least* likely to do so.

Feelings of fulfillment

Those who have ministered to the dying know that there can be intensely gratifying rewards.

Providing comfort and companionship, instead of just physical care, appears to be an important factor in making the task of caring for the terminally ill a rewarding experience.

But not all nurses have experienced satisfaction and fulfillment in caring for incurably ill patients. In fact, almost half seldom or never have had such gratification (see Table 3).

About four out of five nurses who reported feeling almost always or occasionally satisfied and fulfilled, report that they have received strength and support from a dying patient. About two-thirds of the nurses who reported never or seldom experiencing fulfillment reported that they have never received strength and support from a dying patient, indicating perhaps a lack of involvement.

Satisfaction and self-confidence tend to go together: 74% of the nurses who are very confident about their ability to manage the psychological needs of terminally ill patients reported having experienced satisfaction and fulfillment at least occasionally. On the other hand, 72% of the nurses who are slightly confident or not at all confident of their ability to manage the psychological needs, reported having never or seldom experienced satisfaction and fulfillment.

Nurses who have not experienced fulfillment tend to have difficulty in dealing with the families of dying patients. These nurses also are very likely to be anxious and uncomfortable when a terminally ill patient brings up the topic of his death; the nurses' anxiety appears to be strongly related to fear of one's own death.

Nurses who have not experienced fulfillment and satisfaction can't imagine why a nurse would choose to work with the terminally ill. A nurse in a cancer-treatment hospital told us, "One psychiatric nurse who works with chronic schizophrenics commented to me that she didn't know how I could work 'in such a place' with 'such patients' and that I must be terribly depressed all the time. Others feel that I must be a masochist. A child psychologist blatantly told me that I had a warped sense of caring." She goes on to explain, "I enjoy my work immensely, helping patients and families with their cancer, and at times in coping with dying. It's rewarding and fulfilling. Yes, at times it is upsetting and I become very angry at the 'unfairness' of it all. But death is a part of life — something that we have to accept for it will eventually happen to us all one day."

The most distressing patients

The questionnaire asked readers to rate how difficult they'd find coping with their *own feelings* if they were suddenly assigned to care for certain kinds of dying patients. Very few replied that they'd be *unable* to cope with their own feelings, regardless of the patient. But more than half of the nurses said that caring for terminally ill children, adolescents, and mothers with young children would lead to very uncomfortable feelings. Caring for the elderly and middle-aged would produce the least emotional discomfort in nurses. We ranked the responses in order from the most difficult to the least, and they are shown in Graph 2.

A nurse can be very uncomfortable because of a sense of inadequacy; for example, "I have answered 'uncomfortable' but I am uncomfortable only because I cannot do more for them." On the other hand, uncomfortable or not, a nurse may feel quite capable. "Although I'd be 'very uncomfortable' inside with at least my first contacts with many such patients, I 'wouldn't mind' caring for them. I'd support them through the difficult times and learn from the experience," wrote a nurse who is in her 20s.

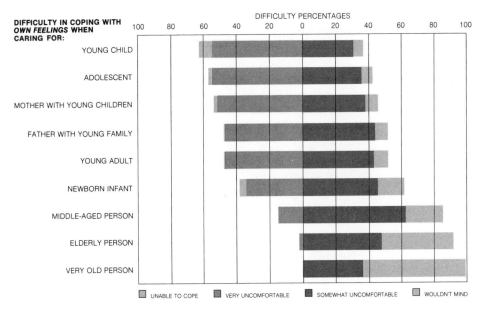

GRAPH 2 — Coping with feelings

And one nurse commented philosophically: "I believe all questions 6 through 14 should be answered the same. Death is and will be the fate of all; we should accept it as such. So why feel differently towards a dying child than you would towards a dying adult?"

Why do more nurses have a more difficult time with young children than with newborns?

One reason is the almost universal feeling of helplessness over not being able to do more. "I can accept the death of an adult," wrote a nurse, "but a child tears me to pieces. They are so helpless and innocent, and have seen so little of life. I cannot comfort a sobbing parent, because I start crying myself and can't speak. I can't cope with it. It's worse since I have two children of my own." An infant, on the other hand, is easier to deal with "because they don't realize what is happening."

Many nurses who are also mothers of young children reported that they sometimes identify too much with young dying patients: "I over-identify between the patient and my own child," and "I would have extreme difficulty caring for an infant or young child because I personally experienced losing a 6-year-old son to leukemia."

What nurses say about distressing patients

"I answered 'wouldn't mind' caring for very old persons. This does not mean I don't care. I do care, but I realize, as do our beautiful elderly folk, that there is a time for us to leave this earth as a part of the natural process of life."
—Respondent #3917

"It is most difficult to deal with the dying so close to my own age. I can rationalize infants' and aged persons' deaths. But I have difficulty coping with that of teenagers and people under 30 who have so much living yet to do. I had less understanding but more acceptance and less fear of death before marriage. Now I have so much to live for that I want to be assured I'll be around for a long time to enjoy it."
—Respondent #9915

Surprisingly, we found that age of the respondent affected the distribution of answers only in a few instances, and that marital status had little or no effect at all.

Age was a factor among young nurses, 17 to 22 years old, to our question on caring for a *dying young adult:* 59% of this age group would find themselves very uncomfortable or unable to cope, as compared to 48% of all older nurses. Nurses over 50, on the other hand, are the most likely to be very uncomfortable in caring for *dying mothers* who have young children, and also in caring for *dying fathers* with young families. There appears to be no age factor at all in distribution of answers to the question about the dying middle-aged patient. Nurses over age 50 do not identify with elderly patients any more than nurses in general do, but young nurses under the age of 28 years tend to be somewhat more uncomfortable in caring for elderly dying patients.

Feelings and specialties

Where a nurse works has more bearing on her ability to cope with care of dying patients than does her age. Pediatric nurses can better cope with death in newborns, for example, than can medical/surgical nurses.

Here are some specific correlations:
• *Care of dying newborns.* Of all respondents, only 18% said they wouldn't mind; but 32% of pediatric nurses and 21% of Ob/Gyn nurses said they wouldn't. Far fewer psychiatric nurses said *they* wouldn't.
• *Care of a dying young child.* Again, pediatric and Ob/Gyn nurses appeared most able to cope with their own discomfort; psychiatric and emergency-room nurses, least able.
• *Care of dying adolescents.* Again, pediatric nurses appeared most able to cope, with ICU/CCU and emergency room nurses higher than average. Medical/surgical nurses appeared least likely to cope.
• *Care of dying young adults and mothers or fathers with young children.* We found minor but no significant differences among nursing groups.
• *Care of dying middle-aged or elderly patients.* Here, too, we found no significant differences. However, geriatric and ICU/CCU nurses appeared slightly more likely not to mind caring for very old persons, whereas psychiatric, pediatric, and Ob/Gyn nurses were less likely. (Interestingly, the psychiatric nurses appear to be more uncomfortable about

death and dealing with terminally ill patients of any age. Is that why they tend to choose a practice where death seldom enters the scene?)

Many nurses wrote that their own emotional discomfort depended largely on the situation and the attitude of the patient.

Sudden death evokes a different set of emotional reactions than death due to prolonged illness. As a medical/surgical nurse put it: "It would depend on why they are dying. It's one thing if a patient is terminally ill with disease, but completely different if he is dying because of, say, something like an auto accident."

Is care of the terminally ill patients more demanding than that of other seriously ill patients? An overwhelming majority — 62% — of respondents said *yes* (24% said *much more* and 38% said *somewhat* more). Another 30% said *about the same.* Only 8% said that the terminally ill patients are *less* time-consuming. Some nurses wrote that the physical care is often less needed but psychological, mental, and spiritual care more needed. Other nurses disagreed, saying that patients usually require more-than-average physical care, but make fewer requests for care.

Do nurses avoid contact with dying patients, sometimes to the point of ignoring their call lights? "Unfortunately, I have found this to be very true," wrote an RN, and 26% of respondents agreed with her. On the other hand 28% of respondents said most nurses go out of their way to give extra care and comfort to dying patients. Another 45% said most nurses treat dying patients about the same as they treat their other patients.

Should priority be given to care of dying patients? We presented the issue in terms of a hypothetical situation: "Do you think Sally is right in giving priority to the care of dying patients?"

The overwhelming response of nurses was *yes* (77%). Many qualified their answers: "Yes, if she has given good care to her other patients and doesn't neglect any of their needs." "Yes, with reservations. As long as critically ill and other patients' needs are not ignored."

Other nurses felt there should be no qualifications. "Absolutely yes," commented an LPN from a medical/surgical unit. A perceptive nurse observed: "It's extremely

What nurses say about care of the dying

"The nurses I work with are unique in their care. If we have a terminally ill patient, we try to arrange our assignments so the nurse assigned to that patient can spend more time with that patient. We all try to assist and encourage both patients and staff when death is imminent."
—Respondent #832

"I've been in rooms of dying patients with RNs running out saying, 'Let's get out of here.
If we're not here we won't see it, and someone else can handle it.' I've heard them say it scares them and seen nurses transfer patients to other floors or units to get away from 'death.' Don't they know none of us escapes death in the end?"
—Respondent #1835

Priority care

What nurses say about care of the dying

"The ideal situation would be this: The patient in a private room where he could be surrounded by his family, not in ICU with its very limited visiting privileges. Drugs to relieve pain and good supportive nursing care, in which the family members are allowed to help. I would encourage the patient and family to speak freely of the impending end of life. Death can be life's last great experience. Some great lessons in courage can be learned from the terminally ill."
—Respondent #840

TABLE 4 — When physicians have refused to tell your patients that they were dying, how many of these patients nevertheless clearly knew of and referred to their impending death? (Q. 33)

Less than 10%	6%
Up to 25%	8
About half	12
Up to 75%	24
Up to 90%	22
Every one, without exception	3
Have not cared for enough dying patients to estimate	25

important to make use of each nurse's individual talents. Sally should be allowed to continue in the wonderful care that she is giving to her two patients because there may be other nurses on the floor that may be incapable of performing this service."

An interesting point was raised by a respondent who claimed, "Many staff supervisors frown on spending time in meeting the psychological needs of the terminally ill." Her letter made us wonder how the answers of nurses in a supervisory position compared with nonsupervisory nurses. For those who said "Yes, Sally is right in giving priority to the care of dying patients," here are the figures: nursing administrators 82%, team leaders 78%, staff nurses 77%, supervisors 75%, head nurses 74%, and assistant head nurses 73%.

Should hospitals have a separate department with a specially trained staff for care of the terminally ill? A majority — 61% — answered *no,* many quite emphatically: "Definitely no!! The dying should never be shoved onto one floor away from the rest of the world."

Some nurses thought that though terminally ill patients should not be segregated into separate wards, each ward should have specially trained nurses to deal with these patients. As one respondent put it, "Not every nurse can (or even wants to) care effectively for these patients."

Nurses who work in small hospitals tended to be more against the idea of a separate department for the terminally ill than nurses in large hospitals. On the other hand, nurses in extended care facilities or nursing homes tended to be more in favor of such a department.

Do patients know?

Some physicians will not or cannot tell patients they have an incurable, terminal illness. Do these patients remain unaware of their impending death even when they are not told? Because

TABLE 5 — In your own experience, how many terminally ill patients continued to deny, until the very end, that they would die? (Q. 34)

Very few, less than 10%...48%
A small proportion, up to 25% 19
About half 7
A large proportion, up to 75% 4
Up to 90% 1
Everyone, without exception 0.05
Have not cared for enough
   dying patients to estimate 21

TABLE 6 — When should a patient with a terminal illness be told that he is dying? (Q. 30)

As soon as possible after diagnosis 60%
Only when he asks 21
Slowly over extended period of
   time as illness progresses...............................16
Never, only that he has
   a serious illness 2
Only in last stages of
   dying when death is imminent 0.5

What nurses say about awareness of death

"I find it sad that terminally ill people who are not told their prognosis must spend their precious few remaining days putting up a front to keep their family and friends assured that they do not 'know.' This is the time that people should be appreciating those close to them, and be becoming even closer to them. This closeness can't be developed in the atmosphere of mutual deceit and secretiveness."
—Respondent #456

"Anselm Strauss says no one should be given a 'death sentence.' There is no pat answer here — it depends on the circumstances of the patient's age, condition, amount of time left, obligations and unfinished business. Even so, if he is told bluntly or gradually, let him retain a glimmer of hope."
—Respondent #10340

nurses are closer to patients, we asked what proportion of the patients seem to see through the attempted deception. Table 4 shows the results.

The more frequently a nurse cares for dying patients, the higher is her estimate: one-third of the nurses who care for dying patients daily said that 90% of the patients knew; 61% said that *at least 75%* knew.

Whether told or not, some patients cannot face their own death and continue to deny it until the end. How many? Table 5 tells the story.

Although apparently rare, denial of death to the very end does occur, and may be useful. A thoughtful nurse, after examining her own reactions, wrote: "Some people do not have the inner strength to face their own imminent death. I think I am one. I would just rather not be told and live with hope to the end of my days."

Almost all nurses who responded, however, feel that a terminally ill patient *should* be told that he is dying. But, as Table 6 shows, there is some difference of opinion as to *when* the patient should be told.

"Soon, sooner, soonest after the diagnosis," declared one respondent. Another pointed out, "Most of them can tell you; you don't have to tell them — we tell them more by what we don't say than by what we do say."

TABLE 7 — When a terminally ill patient brings up the topic of his death or dying, what is your honest inner reaction? (Q. 31)

	ALL RESPONDENTS	NURSES WHO CARE FOR DYING PATIENTS:		
		daily or weekly	twice/month to once or twice/year	almost never
Feel anxious and uncomfortable	15%	14%	15%	20%
Feel somewhat uncomfortable	32	34	32	27
Feel relieved	45	48	46	35
Never involved in such a situation	8	4	7	18

Many felt that the patient should be told as soon as possible, but be given hope. Some respondents combined several answers; for example, "A patient should be told that he is *seriously ill* as soon as possible and, *if he asks,* tell him the prognosis (that he is dying) but also *give hope.*"

Talking with the dying

One might expect nurses who deal with dying patients frequently to be more at ease in discussing death and dying with such patients. Well, it turns out not to be the case. Nurses who deal with dying patients less frequently are just as likely to be at ease in such discussions.

Several interesting details are to be found in Table 7. First, the responses fall mainly into two categories: *uncomfortable* and *relieved.* As long as nurses are involved in providing some care for dying patients, their response to discussing death and dying with a dying patient is much the same, regardless of how often they see such patients. On the other hand, nurses who almost never care for dying patients are less likely to feel relieved when a patient talks of his death.

Feeling uncomfortable when a patient brings up the topic of his death is strongly linked with personal acceptance of one's own death. Two-thirds of respondents who become anxious and uncomfortable when a patient talks of death have not come to terms with fear of their own death or have come to terms only in part. On the other hand, two-thirds of the nurses who are relieved when the patient opens the subject feel that they have come to terms with fear of their own death to a great extent. In addition, nurses who had once felt certain they might die in a relatively short period tend to be less anxious

TABLE 8 — When a patient who has a terminal illness bluntly asks you if he is dying and his physician does not want him to know, what do you usually do? (Q. 32)

Ask why he brought up the question, try to
get him to talk about his feelings 82%
Tell him that only the physician
can answer the question 13
Say you don't know 2
Reassure him that he is not
dying, just ill 1
Avoid the question and
try to distract him 1
Tell him the truth 1

and uncomfortable than nurses who have not.

Age influences attitudes: 57% of the nurses over age 40 feel relieved, and only 8% feel anxious and uncomfortable. More of the young nurses between the ages of 17 and 22 reported becoming anxious and uncomfortable, and fewer reported that they were relieved. Some 16% of the young nurses said they had never had a patient bring up the topic of his death.

Nurses who have never been married are much *more* likely to feel uncomfortable than are married nurses. Divorced and widowed nurses are the *least* likely to feel uncomfortable; more than half (56%) say they are relieved when a patient talks about his own death. The responses of male nurses are similar to those of young nurses.

When is it more difficult to care for a terminally ill patient — when he has been told he is dying or when he has not been told? A great majority of nurses, 85%, say: When the patient has *not* been told. "I'm always afraid that I'll say the wrong thing or act too sympathetic," was a typical comment.

When asked how they'd handle blunt questions from an uninformed patient, most nurses gave the "right" answer — try to get the patient to talk about his feelings (see Table 8). Although this is the approved response to such a situation, it nevertheless is a form of avoiding the basic issue. The patient does not get an answer to his question. "Because of our plastic smiles and sucre bedside manners, we close the door," said one nurse. She went on, "I would like to be free to approach death as openly as possible with the patient. Many physicians and nurses alike try to influence everyone to bury his nose in the sand . . . ."

Some respondents said they'd first refer the patient to the physician, but if the patient didn't get a straightforward answer from the doctor, they'd then take it upon themselves to give

What nurses say about awareness of death

"It seems to me that patients who know everything much more readily adjust to what is going to happen than those who know nothing, but suspect everything."
—Respondent #7271

"I have not met one patient who seems to really buy the idea that the reason they need a colostomy, extensive abdominal surgery, a laryngectomy or radiation therapy is because of 'an inflammatory process.'"
—Respondent #7274

"I don't recall ever being actually forbidden or ordered not to answer a patient honestly when he or she asked about death, but in every single hospital I've worked in, I have always felt that such honesty would cause serious problems for me, and possibly cost me my job."
—Respondent #13328

him the truth. Others wrote that they'd later ask the physician why he didn't tell.

Some nurses have more difficulty dealing with relatives than with the dying patient himself. Discomfort with the parents of dying children was mentioned rather frequently. But 23% of respondents said they usually have no difficulty with relatives, 70% said they have difficulty with some but not with others, and only 7% said they usually find it very difficult.

We found a strong association between a nurse's confidence in being able to handle the dying person's psychological needs and her ability to deal with his family. Little or no difficulty was reported by 88% of the nurses high in self-confidence; great difficulty was reported by 75% of nurses with low self-confidence.

Views on abortion

A Massachusetts RN observed, "There are two 'explosive' subjects woven into this probe, *abortion* and *the right to die*. I have mixed feelings about both issues."

We asked, "Have you ever had an abortion?" Before you go on, stop for a moment and estimate from your own experience (and what you've read) what the general abortion rate for nurses is likely to be. One in a hundred? One in fifty? One in twenty-five? One in ten? One in five? One in three?

Ready? Well, here is the percentage of nurses who responded to this survey who've had an abortion: 11%.

(How does that compare with the abortion rate of American women as a whole? Surprisingly, in spite of careful data collection, particularly by the Planned Parenthood Federation, there are no reliable data on what proportion of American women have had an abortion. The best estimates are from 10% to 25%, at least one abortion.)

Incidence of abortions among nurses over 50 years of age is highest at 17%. Only 8% of the nurses under age 22 say they've had one. For nurses between 22 and 50, the abortion rate is 11%. Separated and divorced nurses show a higher abortion rate than single or married nurses.

Religious denomination also is a factor. Only 8% of the Roman Catholic nurses report having had an abortion, as compared to 11% of the Protestants and about 15% of the Jewish, other, and no-denomination nurses. The more religious a nurse is, the less likely she is to have had an abortion: 5% of the very religious nurses have, 10% of the moderately religious have, 12% of the slightly religious have, and 17% of the not-at-all-religious nurses have had an abortion.

How do nurses feel about having had an abortion? One said, "I've had an abortion but would never go through it again. It's hell once it's over and you have time to think." Others justified their abortion: for example, "I was 18 and unmarried," and "I had to choose between finishing my nursing training and having a baby I didn't want at the time. I have since had three lovely children. . . ."

Three regions differed from the national average (11%) in the percentage of nurses who report having had an abortion: New England (14%), the West (12%), and Canada (7%).

The highest proportion of nurses who *assisted* was in the West (30%), followed by the Southwest and Mountain states (23%). Canadian nurses also are likely to have been involved in an abortion procedure — 25% reported assisting. Nurses in small hospitals, nursing schools, or universities are slightly more likely to have than other nurses.

Rights of the fetus

The future course of legal abortion in the USA is likely to be determined by decisions regarding the rights of the fetus. Judging from the results of our survey, it appears that determining when such rights begin is a *religious* issue more than it is a social, legal, or medical one (see Graph 3, page 164).

As you'd expect, Roman Catholics strongly believe that a fetus has rights either at conception (67%) or when it might be viable outside the womb (23%). But regardless of denomination, *very religious* nurses tend just as strongly to believe a fetus has rights at conception (70%) or when viable outside the womb (19%). (Predictably, the nurses' self-rating of how religious they are corresponds very closely with how frequently they attend church.)

Attitudes toward the rights of a fetus also are very strongly related to a nurse's self-rating of liberalism-conservatism.

Male nurses tend to favor rights at birth more (28%) and rights at conception less (36%) than female nurses. A majority (53%) of nurses under age 22 favor rights beginning at conception. Nurses over age 30 tend to favor rights at birth (23%) more than younger nurses (16%). LPNs and student nurses are the most likely (54%) to say that rights begin at conception. Nurses with a masters or associate degree are the most likely to say rights begin at birth (28%).

What nurses say about abortion

"I am pro-abortion not because I feel a fetus has no rights, but because we are still unable to guarantee his greater rights — the right to be wanted, loved, provided and cared for. I can more easily accept the termination of a fetus that has never known life than see a child whose life has only been one of heartache, neglect and trauma."
—Respondent #12439

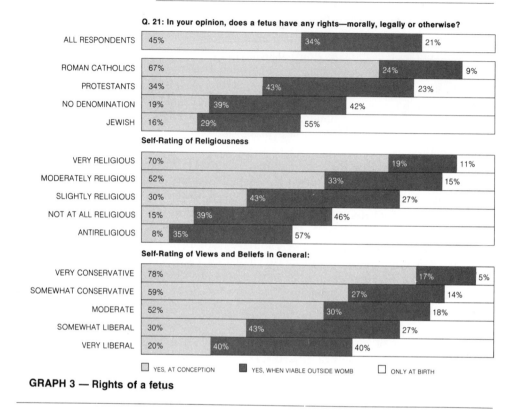

Q. 21: In your opinion, does a fetus have any rights—morally, legally or otherwise?

ALL RESPONDENTS	45%	34%	21%
ROMAN CATHOLICS	67%	24%	9%
PROTESTANTS	34%	43%	23%
NO DENOMINATION	19%	39%	42%
JEWISH	16%	29%	55%

Self-Rating of Religiousness

VERY RELIGIOUS	70%	19%	11%
MODERATELY RELIGIOUS	52%	33%	15%
SLIGHTLY RELIGIOUS	30%	43%	27%
NOT AT ALL RELIGIOUS	15%	39%	46%
ANTIRELIGIOUS	8%	35%	57%

Self-Rating of Views and Beliefs in General:

VERY CONSERVATIVE	78%	17%	5%
SOMEWHAT CONSERVATIVE	59%	27%	14%
MODERATE	52%	30%	18%
SOMEWHAT LIBERAL	30%	43%	27%
VERY LIBERAL	20%	40%	40%

☐ YES, AT CONCEPTION   ■ YES, WHEN VIABLE OUTSIDE WOMB   ☐ ONLY AT BIRTH

GRAPH 3 — Rights of a fetus

Good and bad reasons for abortion?

The nursing profession is deeply divided in feelings about the moral value of abortions. The split occurs along religious lines. Roman Catholic nurses are much less likely to approve of abortion for any reason than are Protestant nurses (see Graph 4). Very religious Protestants, however, disapprove of abortion just as strongly as do very religious Catholics.

Nurses of the Jewish faith generally favor abortion regardless of the reason. Another split also occurs along the liberal-conservative dimension, with conservatives generally against and liberals generally for abortion.

When we asked our computer to find what items in the 70-item questionnaire clustered together in a statistically significant way, it churned out two clusters on the abortion questions: Cluster 1 showing disapproval of "discretionary" abortion and Cluster 2 showing approval of "therapeutic" abortions.

In Cluster 1 — the discretionary reasons for abortion — the

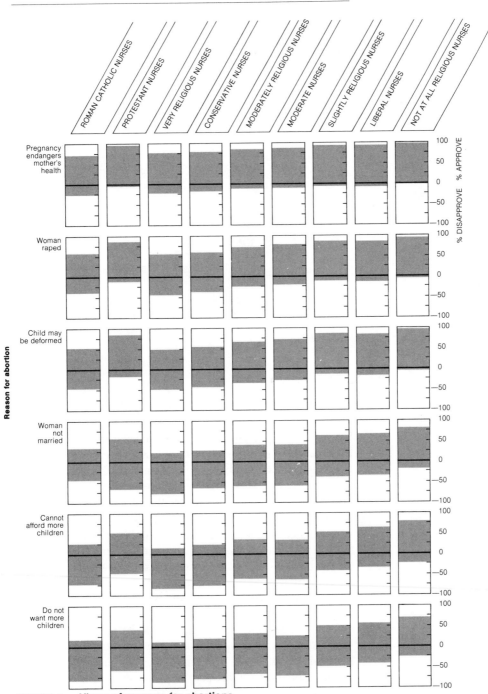

GRAPH 4 — Views of reasons for abortions

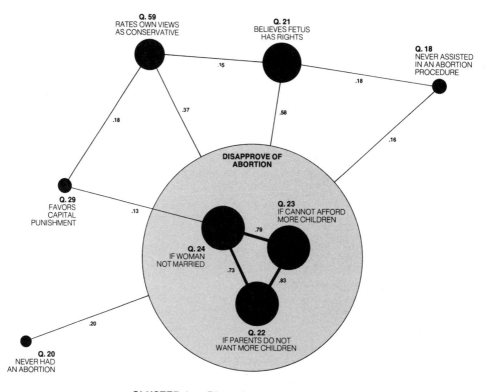

CLUSTER 1 — Discretionary reasons for abortion

strongest influence appears to be what a person believes about the rights of a fetus. Nurses who disapprove of discretionary abortion are likely to believe that fetal rights begin at conception. This in turn is strongly related to the individual's general conservatism and religiousness: the more conservative and religious, the more disapproving of discretionary abortion.

The cluster shows that nurses who *favor* capital punishment tend to be conservative and, surprisingly, tend to favor abortion if the woman is not married. This, at first, appears inconsistent with the overall finding that conservative nurses *do not approve* of discretionary abortion, while liberal nurses do. But further analysis suggests that there is a special subgroup of conservative people who could be called "practical-minded." Although they're conservative, they nevertheless tend to favor abortion for an unmarried woman because the social stigma of bearing a child out of wedlock might ruin her chances for a normal, happy life.

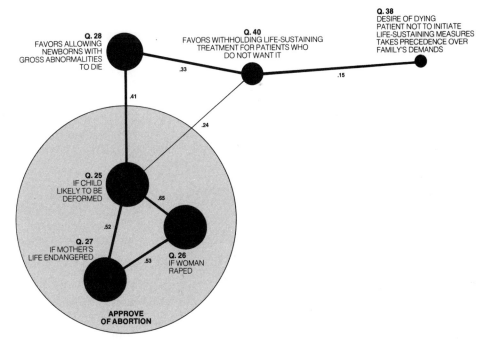

Q. 38
DESIRE OF DYING
PATIENT NOT TO INITIATE
LIFE-SUSTAINING MEASURES
TAKES PRECEDENCE OVER
FAMILY'S DEMANDS

Q. 28
FAVORS ALLOWING
NEWBORNS WITH
GROSS ABNORMALITIES
TO DIE

Q. 40
FAVORS WITHHOLDING LIFE-SUSTAINING
TREATMENT FOR PATIENTS WHO
DO NOT WANT IT

.33

.15

.41

.24

Q. 25
IF CHILD
LIKELY TO BE
DEFORMED

.65

.52

Q. 27
IF MOTHER'S
LIFE ENDANGERED

.53

Q. 26
IF WOMAN
RAPED

**APPROVE
OF ABORTION**

CLUSTER 2 — Therapeutic reasons for abortion

Cluster 1 also shows that nurses who've had an abortion and, to a lesser extent, nurses who've *assisted* in abortion procedures tend to be more permissive in favoring abortion for discretionary reasons.

Cluster 2 deals with the therapeutic reasons for abortion, most of which have been accepted for several decades. Religion and conservatism again are associated with disapproval of therapeutic abortion, but to a lesser extent than with discretionary abortion. The fact that most nurses who responded *approve* of abortion in this cluster indicates favorable views on "merciful deaths" in one form or another.

In a way, abortion may be regarded as a form of mercy-killing — when there is a strong possibility the child will be deformed, or when the life of the pregnant woman is endangered. (In the latter case, the mercy applies to the woman.)

The emotional reaction of women to the possibility of pregnancy through rape is so strong that many favor any means of pregnancy prevention. On the other hand, many letters from nurses pointed out that "almost none of the women who are raped become pregnant."

What nurses say about abortion

"How can nurses refuse to give care to a patient receiving an abortion? Perhaps it is not the same, but would these same nurses refuse to give care to a patient who attempted suicide, an alcoholic going through DTs, or a drug addict going through withdrawal? Abortion is the patient's choice, not the nurses'!"
—Respondent #12379

"Our unit is a surgical unit and quite often we pick up the overflow from our Gyn unit, mostly abortions and tubal ligations. I always regarded these patients as patients. What a shock to realize that my own beliefs regarding abortion *had not affected* my care for these patients, who often need emotional support more than physical care."
—Respondent #910

TABLE 9 — Approval of abortion for various reasons (nurses vs. social workers)

	NURSING74 Respondents approving	TENNESSEE STUDY Nurses approving	Social workers approving
Pregnancy endangers mother's health	88%	92%	96%
Woman raped	78	86	89
Child may be deformed	73	55	82
Woman not married	49	43	63
Cannot afford more children	45	38	63
Do not want more children	39	26	59

Not approving of abortion for rape victims, however, is relatively high among Roman Catholic nurses (39%). But it is just as high among very religious nurses, regardless of religious denomination, and among conservative nurses.

Many nurses pointed out that while they personally disapprove of abortion, they consider abortion a decision to be made by the person involved. Other nurses refused to answer because they so strongly felt that they should not be asked to "approve" or "disapprove" of anyone's having an abortion.

A large number of nurses were against abortion as a form of birth control. "I disapprove if an abortion is the only form of contraception utilized. I approve if the abortion is secondary to a contraceptive device which has failed," wrote one nurse.

A surprising number of nurses favored sterilization, particularly for couples who did not want any more children. Most of the letters talked about *voluntary* sterilization, but not all did: "I strongly feel that sterilization should be *mandatory* for anyone whose life may be dangerously compromised by pregnancy or if the situation were such that succeeding pregnancies would have a strong probability of deformity."

When a mother's life is endangered by the pregnancy, 45% of the nurses who believe that a fetus has rights at conception nevertheless approve of abortion. Approval jumps dramatically (95%) among nurses who believe rights begin when the fetus can become viable and is nearly unanimous (98%) among nurses who believe such rights begin at birth.

The Tennessee Study

A paper on the abortion attitudes of 158 nurses and 419 social workers in Tennessee was published in the May, 1974, issue of

**TABLE 10 — Approval of abortion for various reasons
(nurses vs. public)**

| | NURSING74 RESPONDENTS | | AMERICAN WOMEN GALLUP POLL* | |
	Approve	Disapprove	Approve	Disapprove
Pregnancy endangers mother's life	88%	11%	88%	9%
Child may be deformed	73	27	73	20
Cannot afford more children	45	55	44	50
Do not want more children	39	60	32	64

*1973 Gallup poll. Answers do not add to 100% because "no opinion" responses are not included in the table.

the AMERICAN JOURNAL OF PUBLIC HEALTH. Its authors, G. E. Hendershot and J. W. Grimm, had given questionnaires to professionals in a training program of the Planned Parenthood Association of Nashville. These researchers found that nurses were consistently less likely to approve of abortion than social workers (see Table 9).

The authors raised the question of what implications this might have in abortion services for the poor. They speculated that where nurses do the initial screening of abortion applicants, the nurses' negative attitude may discourage poor women who've been referred to the hospital by social workers.

Various Gallup polls have shown that the public's approval of legal abortion has increased significantly since 1965, and that men favor abortion more than women do. (In our survey, male nurses tended to be slightly more in favor of discretionary reasons for abortion and slightly less in favor of therapeutic reasons than female nurses.)

Unfortunately, the Gallup poll data we have was restricted to white women in America, and we can't assume that black women view the issue in the same way. Also, in our probe, we asked "Do you approve or disapprove?" In the Gallup polls, the question was: "Do you think abortion operations should or should not be legal in the following cases?" Yet, in spite of the differences in the phrasing of the questions, the responses of nurses and of American women in general are amazingly similar (see Table 10).

The Gallup poll found women under 30 years of age more in favor of abortion for discretionary reasons than older women. In our survey, nurses between 23 and 34 years of age also were

TABLE 11 — Have you ever refused to care for an abortion patient? (Q. 19)

Yes, preop only	*1%*
Yes, postop only	*1*
Yes, preop and postop	*2*
No	*53*
Never assigned	*43*

the most likely to approve of abortion for any of the discretionary reasons, but younger nurses — 17 to 22 years of age— tended to be just as disapproving as nurses over 35. Perhaps this reflects their lower likelihood of sexual involvement; women most sexually involved (and hence possibly in need of abortion) tend to be most liberal about abortion.

In the Gallup poll, college-educated women held liberal views on abortion, and to a great extent the same is true of nurses. Associate degree nurses are the most liberal (55% favor abortion when the child is not wanted), followed by nurses with masters degrees (52%) and nurses with bachelors degrees (46%). LPNs are the least likely to approve (29%) of abortion when the child is not wanted, followed by diploma RNs (35% approve) and student nurses (35%).

Care of abortion patients

How about the delivery of nursing care to abortion patients? What sort of care and comfort is a nurse who feels that abortion is a "form of murder" likely to give to an abortion patient?

Nursing74 magazine touched on this in an earlier probe on nursing ethics and found a deep division on the issue, even among nurses who oppose abortion. Some nurses believe they have the right to refuse to care for abortion patients, but a majority of nurses who disapprove of abortion, if assigned, would carry out their duties. The question is, how well?

In the ethics survey, *Nursing74* found that 5% of the respondents *would* refuse to care for an abortion patient if assigned to one; in this survey, we now find that 4% of respondents *have* refused at one time or another (see Table 11). The low rate of refusal among nurses suggests that most nurses who object to abortion, when assigned will care for abortion patients. Such a deduction, however, is misleading. When we looked more closely at the breakdown of the responses, we found that more nurses who disapprove of abortion *have never been assigned* to care for an abortion patient, whereas nurses who approve of abortion are more likely to have been as-

TABLE 12 — How do you feel about withholding all life-sustaining treatment for dying patients who don't want it? (Q. 40)

In favor	73%
Mixed, slightly in favor	23
Mixed, slightly against	3
Against	1

How do you feel about mercy killing or active euthanasia for dying patients who request it? (Q.41)

In favor	17%
Mixed, slightly in favor	31
Mixed, slightly against	16
Against	36

signed. Evidently nurses who disapprove of abortion make their views known and this influences their assignments. Hospital size does not appear to have a great effect on abortion assignments.

More than half of the Roman Catholic nurses have never been assigned, and 6% of the Catholic nurses have refused to care for abortion patients. Only 3% of the Protestant nurses have refused, and most (61%) have never refused such an assignment. Nurses of the Jewish faith are the most likely to have been assigned — in fact all but 16% have.

As you'd expect, Ob/Gyn nurses are the most likely to be assigned to abortion patient care, and 67% of Ob/Gyn nurses have never refused such assignments. But these nurses have a moral conflict on their hands: most (67%) do not approve of abortion for discretionary reasons. These nurses also are less likely to approve of therapeutic abortions than nurses in other specialties. It turns out that Ob/Gyn nurses have the highest refusal rate: 6% have refused to care for abortion patients.

Not surprisingly, Ob/Gyn nurses lead all other nursing specialties in saying fetal rights begin at conception and the least likely to believe that rights begin at birth.

Does a dying patient have the right to refuse treatment? An overwhelming majority of nurses responding to our survey answered, *yes*. But when it comes to active euthanasia or mercy killing, only a minority answered *yes* (see Table 12).

"I believe in allowing the person to die — but not in bringing that death about," wrote one nurse. "We have, with the doctors' knowledge and orders, withheld tube feedings and given just water. Antibiotics have been discontinued, but never, as far as I know, have we actively performed euthanasia."

Conservative nurses and religious nurses tend to be some-

What nurses say about abortion

"Before ever working in Ob/Gyn, I thought of abortion, though legalized in my state, as something done only by prostitutes or 'tramps.' I got a rude awakening. Most abortion patients are not monsters of some sort, but normal people with a variety of reasons. Some are scared teenagers, some of whom don't even want an abortion but are talked into it by parents who can't abide the thought of their daughter getting married at 16 or disgracing the family by having an illegitimate child. I still do not approve of abortion in many instances. But the people who have abortions need a lot of support."
—Respondent #456

Taking away life

"I believe euthanasia is usurping the will of God."
—Respondent #13894

"The act of dying is the most important act of our lifetime and should not be confused with the coward's or defeatist's approach — suicide. The nurse who encourages despair must realize she may be pushing the patient into Hell."
Respondent #7281

"My main objection to mercy killing or active euthanasia is that it simply is illegal."
—Respondent #2828

"Who am I really trying to help — the patient or myself? Am I really running away by promoting mercy killing?"
—Respondent #836

TABLE 13 — What are your feelings about capital punishment? (Q.29)

In favor	*31%*
Mixed, slightly in favor	*31*
Mixed, slightly against	*16*
Against	*22*

what less in favor than liberal nurses of withholding treatment at the dying patient's request and the difference in opinion widens over the issue of euthanasia — mercy killing. Liberal nurses and nonreligious nurses have somewhat more mixed opinions, although on the whole they tend to favor euthanasia for dying patients who request it. We found no significant difference of opinion between female and male nurses.

Does a dying patient have the right to take his own life? Forty percent of our respondents said *no*. A recent nationwide Gallup Poll asked two similar questions — right to end life when suffering from incurable disease, and right to end life if suffering great pain with no hope of improvement. It showed that just over 50% of all Americans believe a person does *not* have the right to end his or her own life; Americans with a college background, however, were less opposed.

Only 14% of our respondents said that the terminally ill patient should be given the means to end his life; most of them said it depended on the patient and the circumstances. An LPN wrote, "I have seen an elderly terminal patient bite through his I.V. tubing to prevent prolonging of the inevitable. I think it was horrible that we drove that man to such extremes."

Not surprisingly, nurses who oppose mercy killing also oppose giving a dying person the means to end his life. On the other hand, only 49% of the nurses who *favored* mercy killing also favored letting the dying patient take his own life; 6% of those who favor mercy killing are opposed to letting the patient do the final job himself.

Here is another paradox: more than half of the nurses who *oppose* mercy killing favor or slightly favor capital punishment. Indeed, it turns out that a substantial majority of all our respondents favor capital punishment (see Table 13).

Conservative nurses are more likely to favor capital punishment and liberal nurses to oppose it. Jewish nurses, contrary to their generally liberal outlook, turn out to be strongly in favor (41%) of capital punishment. Emergency room nurses, perhaps because they see victims of violence

TABLE 14 — Are you in favor or against deliberately allowing newborns with gross abnormalities to die when there is no possibility of any meaningful existence? (Q. 28)

In favor 42%
Mixed, slightly in favor 39
Mixed, slightly against 11
Against 8

more than other nurses do, also strongly favor (41%) capital punishment.

Another aspect of mercy killing involves grossly deformed newborns (Table 14). Care of such infants has in recent years become an increasing problem. A nurse who works in an intensive care nursery wrote: "Many more babies are saved now than would have been just a few years ago. Unfortunately, some of these babies weren't meant to live. Perhaps someday doctors will not try to save every baby born with a heartbeat regardless of how many abnormalities he has."

The great majority of nurses favor letting a deformed newborn die. But many nurses wrote to qualify their approval: "If this means no extraordinary means of assistance, I am in favor. But if it means ordinary means are denied, I am against it."

Feelings about letting deformed newborns die when there's no hope of a meaningful life are strongly related to both the feelings about abortion and about euthanasia. It is, in effect, the connecting link between these two great ethical dilemmas.

When a dying patient wants life-sustaining efforts to stop but his family insists that his life be prolonged, should his desires take priority? Most nurses (96%) believe they should. But in some cases, nurses have to fight their own emotional needs. For example, one nurse described a particularly difficult case. "A stroke patient, previously a robust man, came in comatose. After a week, he showed no response and the family asked that all meds be stopped. It took him 2 more weeks to die. Although none of us believed in prolonging death, it was frustrating not to have our I.V.s, our medications, *to satisfy our needs to be doing something*."

Sometimes a nurse has to face other pressures: "Morally, the patient's desires should be given priority. Realistically, a dead man cannot sue you, nor can he retaliate (unless you believe in haunting). So we often accede to the desires of the

What nurses say about prolonging life

"I believe a person has the right to die with dignity. I work in an ICU/CCU and have walked out of the room several times during CPR when the doctor has us defibrillate the patient 30-60 times and at intervals the patient is alert and begging us to stop to let him die in peace."
—Respondent #6914

"We saved him, if you can call it that. What it amounts to is an ego trip for us."
—Respondent #6925

"Here are my definitions: *Life sustaining* — food, oxygen, general bodily nursing care. *Extraordinary* — I.V., resuscitation, blood transfusion, respirators."
—Respondent #3303

The patient's advocate

TABLE 15 — Have you ever knowingly helped to hasten the death of a terminally ill patient? (Q.44)

Yes, several times, or more	11%
Yes, once	10
No, never	79

family or 'significant others' just to avoid trouble."

On the whole, nurses are against prolonging life by extraordinary means just to study the disease: 77% of our respondents said they are definitely against it, 16% have mixed feelings but are slightly against, 5% had mixed feelings but slightly in favor, and 1% are in favor. One commented, "If the patient while mentally sound agreed to such research, fine! If not, I'm definitely against." Another wrote: "I work in a research unit, and death seems very much like a privilege here at times. These extraordinary means of keeping the heart beating remove any hint of death with dignity."

Some 44% of the respondents said they've worked with doctors and nurses who have hastened the death of a terminally ill patient, but only 21% were willing to admit *they* ever hastened the death of such patients (Table 15).

To many nurses, there's a difference between "hastening" death and "not prolonging" life. As one LPN put it, "Not to prolong life with heroics is not hastening!" A medical-surgical nurse from the Midwest adds: "Pulling out I.V.s or refraining from putting down NGs — I would not call this hastening death but rather refraining from unduly prolonging life." Accordingly, she said she had never hastened the death of a patient.

Some nurses said they have hastened death but only by discontinuing treatments or withholding tube-feeding; other nurses stated explicitly that they have hastened death by giving high doses of narcotics or tranquilizers as ordered by the physician.

Others are careful *not* to do so: "I'd like to comment on the 'morphine' question," one wrote. "It was not covered in your questionnaire but is of deep concern to many nurses. I have refused to give morphine ordered round the clock to a terminal cancer patient whose respirations were depressed. In my conscience, it must be the disease that causes death, not the morphine."

If the needs of the patient come first, there's another side to the "morphine question," which was well expressed in one letter: "I have a number of times administered the order dose of narcotic to dying patients knowing that the medication

TABLE 16 — What is your predominant feeling about having to care for the body of a patient after death? (Q.47)

Acceptance of the necessity of this task 75%
No special feeling 17
Distaste 6
Fear 2

might depress their vital signs enough to hasten death. However, I feel no pangs of conscience for doing so; the dying have the right to leave this world in peace and with dignity, and we must have the strength to allow them to go."

As might be expected, ICU/CCU nurses are the most likely to be involved in situations where they may hasten the death of a patient. Some 20% of such nurses said they have, several times or more, knowingly helped to hasten the death of terminally ill patients.

When it comes to *intentionally* causing the death of terminally ill patients, 9 out of 10 nurses say they have never observed such action by doctors or nurses they work with.

Sociologists find that most people develop generalized anxiety, fear, and disgust when they have to handle a dead body. Nurses, it appears, are not likely to let such feelings overcome them (see Table 16).

"I feel that the body of a patient after death should be cared for with utmost respect and gentleness," a nurse wrote, and her sentiments were repeated in dozens of other letters.

Young nurses (under age 22) are the most likely to experience distaste or fear when caring for a body. A young nurse said simply: "I don't enjoy doing it." Another young nurse said she became depressed and upset.

Nurses over age 40 are the least likely to experience fear or distaste when caring for a body. They apparently have developed ways of handling their emotional reactions. For example, "I find that I have a natural need to care for the body after death as part of my own grieving process," and "It's the feeling of doing one last thing for a good friend."

To what extent have nurses come to grips with the thought of their own death? We found that most have developed a philosophy about their own death, but a substantial minority have not. "I just never give my own death any thought," said one nurse. Another wrote: "Death is the one hurdle I and other nurses have failed to cross and cope with. I can't accept the

What nurses say about their view of death

"Thoughts of my own death aren't frightening, but the way of dying is. So for me, death and dying are two separate issues."
—Respondent #8202

"Most profound experience affecting my attitude toward death: I refused to give a routine (not p.r.n.) dose of morphine to a terminally ill patient who was having Cheyne-Stokes respirations at a rate of two per minute. The next day, the patient, whom I never expected to see again when I left my tour of duty, looked at me in desperation and cried, "Why is it taking me so long to die?"
—Respondent #2380

"Working in a burn unit has changed my attitude toward death. After seeing the suffering of these patients, death now is equivalent in my mind to peace."
—Respondent #11237

Fear of own death

TABLE 17 — Do you feel you have come to terms with your own fear of your own death? (Q.48)

Yes 20%
To a great extent, yes 34
Only in part 33
No 13

reality of my own death at this point (I am 22) and greatly fear it."

Our results (see Table 17) strongly support Dr. Kübler-Ross' observation that a person must carefully consider his own death before he can be comfortable with a terminally ill patient.

As Dr. Kübler-Ross pointed out, experience and maturity are important. Our study showed this in a cross-analysis of age versus coming to terms with inevitability of one's own death. Two-thirds of the nurses over age 35 have come to terms with fear of their own death; younger nurses are most likely to have done so only in part or not at all.

Acceptance of the inevitability of one's own death is highest among very religious nurses: 44% said they have come to terms with fear of their own death, another 37% said they have done so to a great extent, and only 19% said they have not. Nurses who are moderately religious, slightly religious, or not at all religious are less likely to have come to terms with their own death to a great extent (35%) or only in part (35%). Jewish nurses and Catholic nurses tend to fear their own death more than Protestant nurses do. Slightly more males than females have come to terms with fear of their own death.

Imagining the possibility of death is not quite the same thing as being faced with the likelihood of dying in the near future. Indeed nurses who *themselves* have experienced a feeling of imminent death are now less anxious and less uncomfortable in discussing death with terminally ill patients. Also, these nurses find it easier to deal with the family of a dying patient. As might be expected, nurses who have once felt close to dying are more likely to have come to terms with the fear of their own death (see Table 18).

Thoughts of suicide

One-third of the nurses who answered our questionnaire admitted to having seriously thought of suicide at some time (see Table 19). Those who have done so are more likely to have also come to terms, at least to a great extent, with the fear of their own death.

TABLE 18 — Have you ever been in a situation where you were told or felt certain that you might die in a relatively short period of time? (Q. 56)

Yes 28%
No 72

TABLE 19 — Have you ever thought seriously of committing suicide for any reason? (Q. 57)

	Male Nurses	Female Nurses
Yes, many times	6%	3%
Yes, a few times	36	30
No, never	58	67

Male nurses, it seems, are more likely than female nurses to have considered suicide. This finding is quite surprising. Other surveys almost invariably have shown women more likely than men to consider suicide. One possible explanation for the variation among nurses, suggested from studies elsewhere: a relatively large number of male nurses have sexual identity problems. Such problems can trigger suicidal thoughts.

We also found that young nurses (ages 17 to 22) are more likely than the average nurse (5% as compared to 3%) to have considered suicide "many times." But when we looked at the respondents who have seriously considered suicide at all, we found that young nurses don't differ much from the average, but middle-aged nurses (from 29 years to 39) are higher than average: 38% have considered it at least a few times. Nurses over 50 years of age are the lowest — only 27% say they have seriously considered suicide. The lower rate for older nurses suggests that either thoughts of suicide were less common 30 years ago or else older nurses have forgotten such experiences.

Student nurses are particularly likely to have considered suicide — almost half of them (44%) have seriously considered it at least a few times. Associate degree nurses also are particularly likely, 44% having considered it at least a few times.

We found no difference between single nurses and married nurses, but the rate goes up for separated nurses (40% have considered suicide), and up still more for divorced (45%) and widowed (44%) nurses.

The more religious a nurse is, the less likely she is to have considered suicide: of the very religious, 74% never have; of the moderately religious, 69% never have; of the slightly religious, 66% never have. Suicidal thoughts are anathema to very conservative nurses, but apparently not so to nurses with a liberal bent.

What nurses say about suicide

"When I was 20 and rather immature, and thought I might be pregnant, out of wedlock, I seriously considered suicide as the best way out. But only, or mainly, so that my parents would not be disgraced. I wouldn't entertain such an idea now. Even when I'm occasionally depressed it never approaches suicidal feelings."
—Respondent #724

"I would think about committing suicide if I had a terminal illness or would become a burden on my loved ones due to illness or old age. I am a coward and would not want to suffer. I would kill myself in a way that would appear accidental, so there would be no stigma."
—Respondent #1331

TABLE 20 — Nurses who have seriously thought of committing suicide

Hospital administration	50%
Psychiatric	40
ICU/CCU	38
Emergency	38
Pediatrics	33
Medical/surgical	32
Ob/Gyn	30
Geriatrics	29

TABLE 21 — If you were to commit suicide, what reason would be the most likely to cause you to do so? (Q. 58)

Depression and general unhappiness	20%
Intractable pain	9
Terminal illness	8
Generally overwhelmed with problems	7
Rejected by loved one	4
Loneliness	4
Grief at death of loved one	2
Failure or disgrace	2
Insanity	2
Unlikely to commit suicide for any reason	42

TABLE 22 — What does death mean to you? (Q.50)

An ending of earthly life but with the continued individual existence of the soul	43%
Being with God	29
The end of all experiences; a total irreversible blotting out of existence	13
A joining of the soul with a universal consciousness	8
A kind of endless sleep	3
Reincarnation	2
Other	4

Our cross-analysis showed that nurses in some specialties are much more likely to have considered suicide than nurses in other specialties. It gave an interesting spectrum (see Table 20), from which you can draw your own conclusions!

What reasons might drive a nurse to consider suicide? Depression and general unhappiness head the list (see Table 21). Terminal illness and intractable pain come next.

Young nurses, we found, are more likely than older nurses to have considered suicide because of being rejected by someone they love and because of depression.

Beyond death

The majority of all nurses believe in some form of continued existence after death (see Table 22).

We found little difference between the responses of Protes-

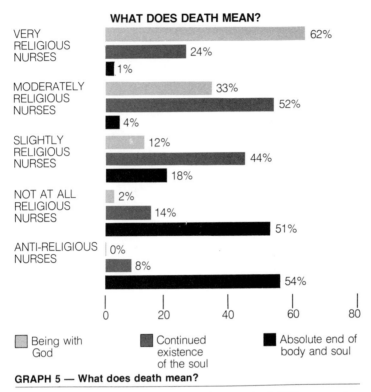

WHAT DOES DEATH MEAN?

VERY RELIGIOUS NURSES
- 62%
- 24%
- 1%

MODERATELY RELIGIOUS NURSES
- 33%
- 52%
- 4%

SLIGHTLY RELIGIOUS NURSES
- 12%
- 44%
- 18%

NOT AT ALL RELIGIOUS NURSES
- 2%
- 14%
- 51%

ANTI-RELIGIOUS NURSES
- 0%
- 8%
- 54%

0   20   40   60   80

☐ Being with God   ◼ Continued existence of the soul   ◼ Absolute end of body and soul

GRAPH 5 — What does death mean?

tant and Roman Catholic nurses, but marked differences for Jewish nurses: 60% of them said that death is the end of one's personal existence. We also found a sharp shift in beliefs as one goes from "very religious" to "nonreligious" (see Graph 5). Nurses who believe death to be the end of a person's existence are more likely than the average not to have come to terms with fear of their own death (28% say they fear their own death). Only 10% of the nurses who believe in some form of afterlife have not come to terms with fear of their own death.

A number of nurses view death as much a part of life as birth is. "When the body dies, the spirit or soul goes on living in another dimension," wrote one. "The *you* of a person goes on living. If this were not so, what would be the purpose of our living or being born?" Another wrote: "Death to me appears to be like birth — but into a much more exciting life." And another saw death as a means of release from "all the cares, frustrations, and worries inherent in living."

Believers in reincarnation are the most likely to have seriously considered suicide (49% of them have). Nurses who

**What nurses say about
their view of death**

"My mother was terminally ill with cancer and came to live with us. I was worried about the effect this would have on my 9- and 10-year-old children, my husband and myself. It was a beautiful experience. My children will never be afraid of death. My husband found a new and demanding role of comforter for me. And for myself, I found peace, satisfaction and a depth of love I didn't know before. The greatest feeling of all came in the last hours before her death."
—Respondent #11357

"My father, who is a very open-minded, analytical type, witnessed the death of a relative, who at the moment of passing became suffused with joy, reached out with her arms and shouted 'Up! Up!' His relating of this incident to me has definitely colored my attitude toward death."
—Respondent #10321

TABLE 23 — Whose death produced the most profound effect on your attitude toward death and dying? (Q. 49)

Patient	25%	Spouse	2%
Parent	22	Son or daughter	2
Grandparent	16	Other	7
Friend	12	Never had such	
Brother or sister	5	an experience	9

TABLE 24 — What has had the greatest influence in shaping your present attitudes toward death and dying? (Q.51)

Religious teaching	32%
Coping with death of someone close	20
Books and articles on death and dying	17
Introspection about own death	14
Conversation with terminally ill patients	11
Conversation with person whose wisdom I respected	3
Other	4

TABLE 25 — What has been your best source of helpful advice and information in learning how to deal with the emotional and psychological problems of dying patients and their families? (Q. 52)

Working and talking with dying patients	38%
Books, magazines	26
Seminars or workshops on death and dying	14
Classes at nursing school	9
Experienced staff member	5
Staff discussions	4
Other	4

believe in the continued existence of the soul or an afterlife with God are less likely to have considered suicide (30%) than nurses who don't believe in an afterlife (42%).

Coping with death and dying

Many nurses become *personally* involved with their patients, and grieve when one dies. "There's a definite sense of loss at the death of a patient; the degree depends upon the length of caring for the patient and the nurse's attachment to the patient," wrote a nurse from Canada. The loss of a family member often affects a nurse's attitude toward dying patients (see Table 23). A nurse from Athens, Georgia, described such an experience: "The lingering dying of my mother from Hodgkin's disease and astrocytoma clarified my feelings and attitudes. This very personal on-going experience has helped me become a better nurse for the terminally ill and their families. I am comfortable in handling their feelings — and confident."

Another nurse wrote, "I recently lost a son, age 21, in a

motor vehicle accident. The feelings elicited from his death were similar to feelings elicited at the death of a patient — except in measure and profoundness."

One-third of our respondents said religion has been the most important factor in shaping their attitudes (see Table 24).

In the "other" category, nurses specified the following: their own near death in an auto accident, their newborn infant, aunt, cousin, uncle, nephew, brother-in-law, sister-in-law, friend's brother killed in Vietnam.

Many nurses ranked several factors as equally important. For example, "Religious teachings and personal beliefs gave me a certain perspective on death and dying. But observing patients go through the process and having them be very frank about their feeling and beliefs have equally helped."

In the "other" category, one nurse reported that her most profound revelations regarding death came "while tripping on mescaline. I felt a complete unity with nature and the universe and realized that nothing is created or destroyed but that its form becomes changed. When I die, the matter of my being becomes the matter of other beings and my soul becomes part of the universal spirit of infinity."

An independent, rather spirited nurse wrote: "I feel *I* am the greatest influence in shaping my feelings on death and dealing with it."

Resources

What primary resources can a nurse draw on to help deal with the pyschological problems of dying patients? According to our respondents, patients themselves are the best resource (see Table 25). Books and magazines were rated high by all nurses except LPNs.

A number of respondents complained about their lack of training in school on caring for the terminally ill. "Thanks for finally admitting that patients do die," said one nurse. "We barely touched on the subject in nursing school, except to be told that we must maintain a 'professional attitude,' whatever that is."

Some nurses, however, did get help from their teachers. One wrote: "The most important source of advice and support for me was my pediatric instructor. She supported me while I was caring for a young child who was dying. When he did die, she allowed me to work out some of my own feelings about death and its sometimes questionable necessity."

*What nurses say about
their view of death*

"Death can be life's last
great experience. Some
great lessons in courage can
be learned from the
terminally ill. I want to go,
as the poet said, 'not like a
quarry slave at night, but
sustained and soothed, as
one who wraps the mantle
of his couch about him and
lies down to pleasant
dreams.'"
—Respondent #840

"Thoughts of my own
death aren't frightening,
but the way of dying is. So
for me, death and dying are
two separate issues."
—Respondent #8202

TABLE 26 — Self-confidence ratings by nurses

	Nursing abilities in general	Provide technical care to terminally ill	Manage psychological needs of terminally ill
Very confident	35%	42%	10%
Mostly confident	59	48	48
Slightly confident	5	8	35
Not at all confident	1	2	7

For some nurses, however, nothing seems to help much. Nurses who admit that they are not confident about their ability to meet the psychological needs of terminally ill patients also admit that they haven't come to terms with the fear of their own death.

Religious beliefs help many nurses in coming to terms with death and dying. In some cases, however, such beliefs may give rise to problems: "My biggest problem in dealing with a dying patient is that if they do not believe in life after death, I find it very hard to give them emotional support."

The kind of nursing education also seems to make a big difference. We found that, in general, the more education a nurse has, the less often she is apt to deal with dying patients — yet the more confident she is of her ability to meet their psychological needs . . . and the more critical she is of other nurses' care of dying patients (perhaps because she escapes the task herself?).

The vast majority of our respondents had a high degree of confidence in their own nursing abilities in general and in their ability to provide *technical* care to terminally ill patients (see Table 26). But not so with ability to manage the *psychological* needs of terminally ill patients. This suggests that some form of additional training, perhaps in the form of workshops or seminars, may be useful to many nurses. For if a nurse is to care for the terminally ill without anxiety and discomfort, she must first come to terms with her own fear of dying.

**Individuals
sharing a challenge**

Can any one nurse fit all of the characteristics and beliefs of our "typical respondent"? No, obviously not, for individuality is the hallmark and the glory of the human race. Just as no grains of sand are exactly alike, neither are people. And so, if you differ in your views from the "typical" respondent to our questionnaire, you are surely typical in doing so.

But facing death and dying in its many forms, as a nurse and as a human — that's the challenge all nurses share.

The goal seems to be that stated by V. Ruth Gray, one of the authors in this book and a nurse especially interested in the death process: "My own personal hope for nurses . . . who care for the dying is this: that we come to accept and understand the fact that physical dying is as much a part of life as physical birth. And when our dying patients say to us, 'Tell me, will I die' we will be able to answer forthrightly, 'Yes, you will, and so will I.'"

For only by coming to terms with the inevitability of her own death can a nurse deal effectively with it in others. For this, some find help in religion, as in *John 3:16*: "For God so loved the world, that He gave His only begotten Son, that whosoever believeth in Him should not perish but have everlasting life."

Others find help in faith, as in Kelly's A TESTAMENT OF DEVOTION quoted in Chapter 1 of this book: "Life from the beginning is a life of unhurried peace and power. It is simple; it is serene; it is amazing; it is triumphant. It takes no time, but occupies all our time and makes life's programs new and overcoming. You need not get frantic, for He is at the helm, and when your little day is past, you lie down quietly in peace, for all is well."

And some rely on philosophy, as expressed by Edward Young, in the 16th century:

Death is the crown of life;
Were death denied, we all would live in vain;
Were death denied, to live would not be life;
Were death denied, ev'n fools would wish to die.

Skillcheck answers

SKILLCHECK 1

- Helen may be in the stage of anxious denial. The doctor's message may not have begun to penetrate her consciousness because she isn't ready to consider the possibility of death.
- Helen may have misunderstood the doctor's message.
- Helen probably has a deep concern for her children's welfare. She also may be displacing some of her anxiety over her condition onto them.
- She may be testing your reaction in an effort to refute the doctor's message.
- Helen may be making a disguised plea for help in coping with her feelings about death.

Situation 1 — Helen

- Don may be in the depression stage. His withdrawal could be a sign of his first realization that he may die and lose the things he loves.
- Don may have passed through the other stages of grief and now be in the stage of acceptance. He may be emotionally separating himself from the world around him in preparation for physical separation.
- If Don is in pain and discomfort, he may be conserving all of his energy to deal with his physical condition.
- Don may be withdrawing because he resents his dependency on others and feels worthless.

Situation 2 — Don

- Maggie may be in the anger stage — the reality of her terminal condition may have finally penetrated her consciousness.
- Because Maggie has lost control of her life, she may be trying to regain some sense of control by trying to assert herself as "superior" to you.
- Maggie may be angry because she actually wishes that *she* could be too busy to read. Your question may have aroused her resentment and anger over the vitality she has lost.

Situation 3 — Maggie

- Louise's comment may indicate that she's maintaining hope.
- Louise may be denying the possibility of death by identifying with her friend, even though her friend's condition was not exactly like hers.
- She may be testing your reaction.
- Louise may not understand the seriousness of her illness.

Situation 4 — Louise

- John may be in the stage of bargaining. He may be trying to win a reprieve from God by reading the Bible and performing "good deeds" (promising his body to science).
- Because John thinks that nurses and doctors can save his life, he may be bargaining for your help by trying to win your approval and praise.
- John may have come to grips with his situation through religious faith.
- Having realized that death is imminent, John may be performing altruistic deeds to "win a place in heaven."
- He may be willing his body to science in an effort to retain some control over his body after death.
- John may be expressing a wish for immortality by arranging for some parts of his body to "live on."
- John's former hope that he'll overcome his disease may have been replaced with the hope that his organs can help someone else.

Situation 5 — John

- Mr. Jennings may be in the bargaining stage. He may be trying to

Situation 6 — Mr. Jennings

postpone death by promising to accept his plight if allowed "a little more time."
- Mr. Jennings may have accepted the inevitability of death but may feel that he must attend to this last bit of unfinished business (his grandson's marriage) before he can let go.
- Mr. Jennings may be focusing on life-affirming events and trying to demonstrate his stamina in an effort to deny the threat of death.
- He may be testing you to get some idea of how long he has to live.

Situation 7 — Mrs. Graham
- Mrs. Graham may be displacing her anger over her situation onto you.
- Mrs. Graham may resent your presence because it reminds her of the daughter she will have to give up.
- Mrs. Graham may feel frightened and helpless because she sees her situation as a role reversal, where she is the child and you (representing her daughter) are the parent.
- Mrs. Graham may feel that, as a student, you don't have enough experience to care for her properly. She also may be distrustful because she has had negative experiences with other student nurses.

Situation 8
Read your essay and analyze your reactions. Ask yourself the following questions:
- What kind of feelings did you have deep inside?
- Were you tempted to make light of the patient's statement? To give him quick reassurance?
- Did you wish that you had left his room for last? Did you look for an excuse to leave quickly?
- Did you wonder if you would get your work done and get off in time?
- Did you try to determine what resources you could use to help the patient cope with his feelings?
- Did you recognize the hint of loneliness in his statement? Did you try to deal with it, rather than trying to quiet him with a drug?
- Did you accept his statement as possibly intuition, realizing that people usually have a "sense" about their death?

SKILLCHECK 2

Situation 1 — Mr. Schwartz
- If you have a close relationship with the family, you might sit down privately with them and comment on what a terrible ordeal this must be for them. Mention that you've noticed that they seem to be having more difficulty accepting the situation than Mr. Schwartz. In this way, you can encourage them to grieve with you rather than with the patient.
- Or, if you have a very close relationship with the family and know they won't resent your interference, you might be able to explain honestly but nonjudgmentally that they are putting Mr. Schwartz in a bind. Explain that, in order for Mr. Schwartz to die peacefully, they need to "let go."
- Or, if one member of the family seems to accept the situation better than the others, you might take him aside and ask how he thinks both of you could help the family to come to grips with Mr. Schwartz's condition.
- In any case, you could make yourself available to the family whenever they feel the need to express their grief. Encourage them to express their needs to you rather than to the patient.
- You also might ask a clergyman to see if he could help them express their grief and cope with the situation.

Situation 2 — Mrs. Young
- You should listen carefully to Mrs. Young and simply give her the freedom

to express her feelings through crying, screaming, or other ways. If touch seems appropriate, hold her hand or put your arm around her.

- When the first wave of grief subsides, you might comfort her by saying, "You and your husband had fights before and you always made up. I'm sure he knew how deeply you loved him."
- After the body is prepared, you could ask Mrs. Young if she would like to spend some time alone with her husband. Often relatives will privately express their feelings and make apologies to the deceased if they can sit alone with him for a short time.
- After a sudden death, true mourning usually starts nearly a week later. If you had established a close relationship with Mrs. Young previously, you could call or write her at home in a couple of weeks to ask how she is doing. This would open the door to further communication.

Situation 3 — Bobbie

- You should make an effort to establish a rapport with the parents so they will feel comfortable with you. If you succeed, you might try to explain your concern for them and for Bobbie.
- You might ask the physician to talk to the parents with you. That way, you could make sure they are hearing what the doctor tells them.
- Or, if you don't feel you would be betraying Bobbie's trust, you could share with them the conversations that you've had with Bobbie that have indicated she knows her condition and needs her parents' support to confront it. If Bobbie has expressed her understanding through drawings, you could share them with the parents too.
- If the parents still refuse to face the situation, you should make a concerted effort to avoid judging their behavior or projecting your own values on them. Don't reject them if they aren't able to deal with this situation more effectively. Rejecting them will only make the situation worse for Bobbie.

Situation 4 — Mrs. Washington

- You could answer, "You've been a very devoted and loving family during this terrible ordeal. Yes, she did call out for her youngest son and did seem to be in some pain. But we made her death as comfortable and peaceful as possible."
- Or you could say, "I know it must be very upsetting for you to have spent so much time with her and not to have been here when she died. But we did all anyone could to make her comfortable."
- Or you could say, "I know how upset you must be to have been away when she died. But she knew how much you loved her and I'm sure she knew that you were close by."

Situation 5

Read your essay and ask yourself the following questions:
- Did you appreciate that this girl had chosen you to share her spiritual confusion and torment?
- Were you tempted to call a clergyman right away?
- Did she cause you to question your own religious beliefs?
- How do you envision a human being and your responsibility for a person's care? Do you see a person as a combination of body and soul?
- What does total patient care mean to you?
- Do you think the spiritual dimension greatly affects a person's health?
- Do you think guilt affects healing?

Situation 6

Read your letter, answering the following questions:
- Did you find yourself using platitudes?
- Did you communicate your honest feelings and beliefs?
- Were you tempted to put off writing the letter until later?

- Did you consider what you would like someone to say to you if you were receiving a letter of condolence?
- Did you recognize that the letter wouldn't excuse you from personal contact with the bereaved?

SKILLCHECK 3

Situation 1 — Dr. Greenberg

- After making rounds with Dr. Greenberg, you could comment on how tough working with dying patients must be. This would give him the opportunity to express how he feels. If he opened up and you had a very close relationship with him, you then might be able to gently mention how he comes across to others.
- Or you could ask to speak with him privately and reverse roles. You could tell him that *you* have trouble dealing with death and dying and find yourself being abrupt with patients and co-workers. If he admits having the same difficulty, you can ask how both of you could overcome it. Or, if he doesn't admit having the same difficulty, you could ask for his suggestions on how to overcome it. Perhaps by helping you, he will help himself.

Situation 2 — Mrs. Marks

- You could inform the doctor that Mrs. Marks is asking the staff very direct questions, hoping that he will reconsider his decision.
- You could also visit Mrs. Marks frequently. Instead of waiting for her to ask a question that you can't answer, though, you could ask her questions such as, "Rough day today?" That way, you can let her know that you understand her feelings and give her the chance to express them.
- If Mrs. Marks asks you directly for her diagnosis and prognosis, you could tell her that only her doctor can answer that question. But you also could say that you'd be more than willing to talk with her about any problems she's having.
- You could also ask for a staff conference to get the group's support and insight into ways to handle the situation.

Situation 3 — Mrs. Hansen

- You could discuss the situation with your head nurse or a clinical specialist, explaining your strong feelings of identification. If this didn't ease your encounters with Mrs. Hansen, you could ask not to be assigned as her primary nurse. However, you should continue making short visits so she doesn't feel rejected.
- You could regard this as an opportunity to have "one last chance" to do something good for your mother.
- You could tell Mrs. Hansen about your mother and that she reminds you of her. Perhaps she will say that you remind her of someone very close to her. In any case, getting your feelings into the open and discussing them with Mrs. Hansen may make the situation less difficult for you.
- If you have had this experience before, you should realize that similar situations will probably continue to arise if you don't resolve your feelings about your mother's death. You might consider professional counseling to explore and come to terms with your feelings.

Situation 4 — Staff Morale

- If your hospital has a nurse specialist in death and dying, you could ask her to conduct group meetings where everyone could "mourn" the loss of patients.
- You could also hold weekly meetings so that the staff would become sensitive as a team to the needs of patients and each other.
- You could also suggest that the staff do something good for itself — go out to dinner together, have a coffee-and-cake break one morning, have a party.

- If you really feel that Rev. Sanders has accepted death and you have a good relationship with him, you could tell him honestly about your difficulties accepting his situation. This could open the door to a frank discussion that could be extremely enriching for both of you.
- If your hospital has a clinical specialist or nurse specialist in death and dying, you could explain your feelings to that person. Perhaps she could help you understand your difficulties and give you some hints on how to cope.

Situation 5 — Rev. Sanders

Analyze your essay for the following:
- What does it reveal about your general attitude toward death?
- Did you use the pronoun "I" or did you try to evade thoughts of your own death by using words like "people" and "you"?
- Do you feel that your views are the only "correct" ones, or are you willing to accept different views from others?
- Did you talk about what you consider basic rights for each human being in death and dying? If not, write another essay outlining your ideas on the following:
- How do you feel about prolonging death?
- Do you think a person has a right to die as well as to live?
- Could you "pull the plug"?
- Who should be present when life-support systems are terminated — family, doctor, nurse, clergy, social worker, others?

Situation 6

Think about your reactions to this exercise.
- Were you able to picture yourself as dead?
- Were you actually able to write a full paragraph about your feelings? Were you sidetracked by noises or movements around you? Did you welcome distractions?
- How long did the time seem?
- If you found focusing on your death for a few minutes difficult, try to imagine what a terminally ill patient experiences.
- If you found this exercise easy, try it again for a longer period — concentrating on your own death for 5 or 10 minutes.

Situation 7

Reread your essay. Then, think about the following:
- What would you like said about you?
- What kind of eternal truths give you comfort?
- Do you have any strongly positive or negative feelings as you read your own name in this kind of context?
- What new priorities does this exercise suggest that you set for yourself?

Situation 8

Index